ON TARGET

Bible-Based Leadership for Military Professionals

Paul D. Cairney

authorHOUSE®

AuthorHouse™
1663 Liberty Drive
Bloomington, IN 47403
www.authorhouse.com
Phone: 1-800-839-8640

First published by AuthorHouse   11/11/2010

ISBN: 978-1-4520-7231-9 (e)
ISBN: 978-1-4520-7230-2 (sc)

Printed in the United States of America

This book is printed on acid-free paper.

AKNOWLEDGEMENTS

I want to first acknowledge our gracious God who has called me, in spite of my shortcomings, to lead in the United States military. This project actually started during my final semester at the United States Air Force Academy in the spring of 1992 when I first started contemplating how a leader in the military should seek to glorify God. I hope this project is useful to those who want to glorify God as they honorably and sacrificially serve their country in the armed forces, and I pray that this project honors the God who has called each of us to lead. I want to thank Dr. Neal Weaver for giving me the opportunity to explore this lifelong interest with such freedom. I want to also acknowledge Dr. Steve Thurman, a pastor, mentor, and personal friend, who has an incredible passion for Christian leadership and has been such an inspiration to me as I started and worked through this project; he is a pioneer in this work who has literally had an international impact by inspiring those called to serve the Lord through leadership. I also want to thank my parents, Dr. William and Linnea Cairney who encouraged me in my work, and especially my Dad who gave so much of his personal time to edit and critique my work. Finally, I want to thank my dear wife, Lynn Marie, the love of my life who has patiently sacrificed the many long hours I have given as a leader in the military as well as those I needed to devote to this project. You have been a constantly encouragement to me through it and I could not have completed this without your support, Sweetheart! I love you!

Soli Deo Gloria!

INTRODUCTION

August 2010

When I began putting together my dissertation for my doctoral studies at Louisiana Baptist University, I had two goals in addition to getting it accepted so I could graduate. First, I wanted to write something that was not purely academic, but something that people would actually want to read and enjoy reading. Second, I didn't want to write something purely theoretical, but rather something practical and applicable to leaders in the military as well as for leaders in any vocation. This is also why I decided to publish my dissertation, because no information, however profound, is any good if it is left on a university library shelf collecting dust. With the exception of some minor formatting changes, what you are reading is my dissertation as submitted to Louisiana Baptist University in 2007. I have added a few thoughts and some historical examples to it, as well as successes and failures from my own experience which can help illustrate the points I am making in the text. My hope and prayer is that this book will help guide other leaders who, like me, yearn to be the leaders God intends us to be.

Paul D. Cairney, PhD
A leader in the making

CONTENTS

PART I
Intimacy With God Is The Key To Successful Leadership

Throughout the Scriptures, there is a consistent theme in the exercise of any spiritual gift in general and the gift of leadership in particular. As God calls leaders to exercise their gift and execute the mission, He has one prerequisite in place, and this He states loudly and clearly. This prerequisite is an intimacy with God. God clearly blesses the leadership efforts of those who establish and maintain a close relationship with him; likewise God does not bless, indeed He often frustrates, the efforts those whom He calls to leadership but do not maintain a close relationship with Him. Clearly, intimacy with God is the key to successful leadership.

CHAPTER 1
Intimacy with God is a Prerequisite to Spiritual Gifts in General

(Matthew 22 and Romans 12)

The call to intimacy with God is first of all foundational to discipleship in general, even before the exercise of spiritual gifts comes into question. In Matthew 22, Christ makes it very clear that without a deep love for God all else is lost, making the question of spiritual gifts purely rhetorical. When asked what the most important commandment in all the Torah was, Christ responded by stating:

> You shall love the LORD your God with all your heart, with all your soul and with all your mind." This is the first and greatest commandment. And the second is like it: 'You shall love your neighbor as yourself.' On these two commandments hang all the Law and the Prophets. (NKJV)[1]

Loving God was and is the very crux of everything God calls his people to do. Without this love for God, all else God would call his people to do would fall, and this would include the use of any spiritual gift. It is absolutely foundational.

This passage also gives a good description of what this love for God actually is. Eugene Peterson's paraphrase makes this love even more intense: "Love the Lord your God with all your passion and prayer and intelligence" (*The Message*).[2] It is a deep and burning commitment God calls us to. It is also singular – it is "to be directed wholly and exclusively to Yahweh, not shared with false Gods."[3] It is a love which also "finds expression in consistent obedience to Yahweh's commands"[4] – in other words, it is one of action not just of feeling. It is also a love involving the whole person;

"a person must love God with his whole being, with every capacity at his command."[5] As Matthew Henry stated,

> Our love of God must be a sincere love, and not in word and tongue only. It must be a strong love, we must love him in the most intense degree. It must be a singular and superlative love, we must love him more than anything else; this way the stream of our affections must entirely run. The heart must be united to love God, in opposition to a divided heart.[6]

This deep, passionate love is the intimacy God calls his people to.

As a foundation for the entire Christian life, then, an intimacy with God is essential. It is also essential, more specifically, in the use of spiritual gifts. Chapter 12 of Paul's epistle to the Romans is well known for its discussion of spiritual gifts, including the gift of leadership. However, just as important as his analysis of the gifts he lists in this chapter is the foundation he lays for their use in the first two verses of the chapter which gives further insight into the intimacy God desires of his people.

> Therefore, I urge you, brothers, in view of God's mercy, to offer your bodies as living sacrifices, holy and pleasing to God—this is your spiritual act of worship. Do not conform any longer to the patterns of this world but be transformed by the renewing of your mind. Then you will be able to test and approve what God's will is—his good, pleasing and perfect will (NIV).[7]

Paul here is stating two needs of any saint who desires and is called to exercise a spiritual gift. The first need is a complete dedication to God, without condition and without exception. Matthew Henry wrote that Paul's use of the word "body" is not limited to the physical body of the saint but of the entire person, an echo of Matthew 22. "The presenting of the body to God implies not only the avoiding of the sins that are committed with or against the body, but the using of the body as a servant of the soul in the service to God."[8] Indeed, the sacrifice of ourselves to God and to his work must be an act of the deepest recesses of the heart and of the will. Henry continues, "There must be a real holiness which consists of an entire rectitude or heart and life, our bodies must not be made the instruments of sin and uncleanness but set apart for God."[9]

This act of sacrifice is one, according to Marshall Pickering, that does not happen all at once, but is a constant and on-going act of the will of the believer:

In urging his readers to 'offer' themselves to God, Paul exhorts them to place themselves at his disposal, for they are his property as much as were the sacrifices in Old Testament worship, and the sacrifices are to be continually repeated as living, holy, and 'pleasing to God' in free and personal surrender. This constitutes spiritual worship, or better, the 'logical' action of worshiping, that requires a conscious, rational, thoughtful, and intelligent offering of the self in daily sanctification that is in God's sight pleasing.[10]

Barton and Muddiman agree. They write, "Offering 'your bodies a living sacrifice' connotes giving oneself continuously and entirely. Any lesser response misprizes the greatness of God's own offering."[11] In other words, to exercise a spiritual gift, the believer must completely dedicate himself to God, a dedication which takes regular and purposeful renewing. "At root, the Christian life is one consecrated to God,"[12] wrote Gutherie and Motyer, and this consecration is the essential foundation to any work for and with the Holy Spirit.

This dedication is not only one of depth but of breadth as well, touching every part of an individual's life. Eugene Peterson paraphrases this passage as such: "Take your everyday, ordinary life – your sleeping, eating, going-to-work, and walking-around life – and place it before God as an offering. Embracing what God does for you is the best thing you can do for him" (*The Message*).[13] It is a complete dedication Paul asks for, not just of everything we are but of everything we do.

The second need Paul states is the need to not be conformed to this world, or "do not live according to the style or manner of this present age."[14] In other words, Paul exhorts us to think in a way which is God-driven and not driven by popular thought. This is especially true in leadership. As leadership fads come and go, a leader must focus on what God desires of His leaders, not so much to exclusion of popular thought but in primacy over popular thought. God's thoughts on leadership may be in agreement or in contradiction to current leadership philosophy, but we must always follow God's ways instead of that which the world dictates; God calls us to a discretion that knows the difference between God's ways and the world's ways. Peterson paraphrases it,

> Don't become so well-adjusted to your culture that you fit into it without even thinking. Instead, fix your attention on God. You'll be changed from the inside out. Readily recognize

what he wants from you, and quickly respond to it. Unlike the culture around you, always dragging you down to its level of immaturity, God brings the best out in you, develops well-formed maturity in you. (*The Message*)[15]

Instead of conformity, Paul calls all who exercise a spiritual gift to "be transformed by the renewing of your mind." Just as the offering of oneself as a sacrifice to God, Charles Ryrie notes that this is not a one-time change but a "continual process of change from the inside out."[16]

The result of the nonconformity and transformation is the ability that the saint will have to "test and approve what God's will is – his good, pleasing and perfect will." This means that we will be able to understand and do precisely what God calls us to do in the exercise of our gifts. It is this nonconformity and transformation which allows us to use the spiritual gifts given by God for God's purposes, rather than for any purpose of worldly or selfish gain. "By the will of God," wrote Henry, "we are here to understand his revealed will concerning our duty, that will which we pray will be done with us as it is done by the angels."[17]

The essence of this passage is a clear message that we cannot have this ability to know and do what God's will is in the exercise of spiritual gifts without the dedication to God Paul calls us to. The construction of this passage demonstrates that the offering of our whole selves coupled with the nonconformity to the world and transformation of our minds are preconditions to the ability to know and do God's will. The single word "then" clearly indicates that only if we are committed to this continual process of change away from worldly thoughts to Godly thoughts will we be able to execute what God desires. Ryrie succinctly says, "Dedication gives the ability to discern God's will."[18] Without that dedication, we simply cannot do what God desires. This is the intimacy with God that we are called to – the closeness to God which allows us to know his thoughts and desires.

As much as this intimacy is necessary for the use of a spiritual gift, there is also clearly a significant danger when a saint attempts to exercise a spiritual gift without that intimacy with God. In fact, one could argue that without intimacy, we cannot exercise a spiritual gift and that any activity we do, even in the name of God, is inherently unspiritual and ungodly. This is sadly a common situation. Henry and Mel Blackaby state, "Christians are seeking gifts of the Holy Spirit and not the Holy Spirit Himself. They want power but not a relationship with the One whose presence gives power."[19] What this is, then, is a contradiction – spiritual gifts without the Spirit

Intimacy or activity?

So far as I know, I am the only security forces officer in the US Air Force who also possesses a seminary degree. The masters degree program I did through Liberty University was excellent. It was long – it took me over seven years to complete it as an external degree program – and I felt a great sense of satisfaction when I completed it. Still, I realized something was missing as I was in the midst of the program and it didn't take me too long to figure out what was wrong – I had let God become academic. Although my intent to do this degree program was good, God had become a matter of theology, apologetics, and hermeneutics to me, not the living and powerful God who had a vested interest in who I was. I had, as John wrote to the church in Ephesus, lost my first love. I was knowing about God, but not knowing God. I had to focus more on God himself and re-establish my relationship with Him. Don't get me wrong, the activity I was doing was good and God's will, but I had lost my focus. Any endeavor, however noble or spiritual, can also lead us away from our relationship with Christ, even pastoring a church, leading a Bible study or joining the choir. In fact, it is very possible that people are afraid of intimacy with Christ and use these activities as a substitute for the intimacy God is seeking in us. Activity is never a substitute for a real relationship with God, however good that activity may be. This is especially true of leaders. However important your endeavor, it is no substitute for intimacy with Christ.

who gives them, which according to the Blackabys is logically impossible. "We must learn to understand," they write, "that there are no gifts apart from an intimate relationship with the Spirit."[20] They state emphatically, "We must understand a simple principle: *If you do not walk in the Spirit, you do not have a spiritual gift.*"[21] In other words, the intimacy that Paul calls us to is far from optional—there is no use of any spiritual gift without the intimacy essential to the exercise of it.

This makes logical sense as well. If a spiritual gift is a manifestation of the power of the Holy Spirit, then that manifestation is only present when called upon by the Holy Spirit. "You cannot convince the Holy Spirit to do what He doesn't want to do," state the Blackabys, "and He always wants to do the Father's will. In other words, if you're living outside His will, it's impossible to function according to any 'spiritual gift' you may think you have, for you aren't walking in the Spirit."[22]

The lack of intimacy not only makes any Godly service impotent, it is also a liability since our actions are then contrary to the will of God; what would have been a spiritual gift, if not governed by the Holy Spirit through intimacy with God, becomes destructive. As John Borek, Danny Lovett, and Elmer Towns stated, "The absence of Godly character in Christians has a tendency to weaken the impact of Christianity in society."[23]

Ironically, often those who allow this to happen are the ones who appear to be the most spiritual. It is far too easy to substitute activity for the intimacy which God so clearly requires; our ministries and activities take primacy over our love for God. This, though, cannot be; intimacy must come first. Rick Bereit states clearly, "Above all we are to love God… However, activities are not a substitute for loving God. Our love for God is the fuel that powers the activities."[24] Intimacy with God must come before any exercise of spiritual gifts, and that order must be feverishly maintained. Bereit continues,

> There is no substitute for loving God—not sharing the Gospel, not leading people to Christ, not religious activity, not lengthy time in prayer. These activities flow out of a love relationship with God. No activity and no person should have the place of affection in our souls that is God's.[25]

Os Guinness also agrees that there is a specific order in our calling from God – the calling to intimacy with Him, followed by the calling to the exercise of the spiritual gifts.

> Our primary calling as followers of Christ is by him, to him, and for him. First and foremost we are called to Someone (God), not to something (such as motherhood, politics, or teaching) or to somewhere (such as the inner city or Outer Mongolia). Our secondary calling, considering who God is as sovereign, is that everyone, everywhere, and in everything should think, speak, live, and act entirely for him…This vital distinction between primary and secondary calling carries with it two challenges – first, to hold the two together and, second, to ensure that they are kept in the right order. In other words, if we understand calling, we must make sure that first things remain first and the primary calling always comes before the secondary calling.[26]

The Blackabys agree as well, that intimacy with God must be preeminent. "God," they write, "created you with your unique abilities, and He does want you to use them. But He's far more interested in you knowing Him than He is in knowing your abilities."[27]

Rick Warren, in his Number One New York Times Bestseller book, *A Purpose Driven Life*, sums up the thought of intimacy with God very well. He states,

> Much confusion in the Christian life comes from ignoring the simple truth that God is far more interested in building your character than he is anything else. We worry when God seems silent on specific issues such as 'What career should I choose?' The truth is, there are many different careers that could be in God's will for your life. What God cares about most is that whatever you do, you do in a Christlike manner.[28]

> Charles Stanley echoes his words:

> In order to experience intimacy with the heavenly Father, you must genuinely regard Him as more important than everything else you pursue in life. It is important to have goals and relationships, but your primary pursuit should be to know God.[29]

There is no doubt, then, that intimacy with God is essential to the exercise of spiritual gifts. Nothing can be a substitute for that intimacy. Without it, anything we do is contrary to the will of God and becomes disruptive to what would otherwise be Godly actiities.

CHAPTER 2
Intimacy With God Is Essential For Leaders

While intimacy with God is a prerequisite to the use of any spiritual gift, it is especially essential when applied to leadership. The leader who neglects to find or maintain intimacy with God will be less effective and possibly destructive in his or her endeavors, while the leader who sets his heart to establish and maintain intimacy with God will find himself very effective. Oswald Sanders wrote, "As the leader gives control of his life to the Spirit, the Spirit's power flows through him to others."[30]

Intimacy with God is the foundation of character, which any aspiring leader must have. As Borek, Lovett, and Towns wrote, "While leadership principles are important, character is essential."[31] This stands to reason – leadership is influence,[32] and a leader sets the moral and ethical tone of any organization; what the leader exemplifies the organization will inevitably emulate.

A leader who exemplifies character will lead an organization of integrity and high ethical behavior, and what leader does not want this? Yet it is solely up to the leader to set the tone and example for the remainder of the organization. Whether in Christian circles or not, character is absolutely essential. Kouzes and Posner wrote,

> Somewhere along the way to the New Millennium notions of ethics, morality, honesty, character and personal discipline came to be viewed as quaint—at least by those from a me-first, free agent school of corporate strategy...Certainly the context of leadership has changed, but given what we've all experienced, we've come to see how necessary it is to be reminded of some fundamentals which do not change. Fundamental number 1: Character counts.[33]

The opposite is true as well. The leader who exemplifies a lack of character in his own behavior, whether on purpose or not, will find the same lack of character among the people in his organization. As Sanders wrote, "If those who hold influence over others fail to lead toward the spiritual uplands, then surely the path to the lowlands will be well worn."[34]

> **The Ideal Leader?**
> One exercise I have done as I have taught leadership is to have the class brainstorm qualities leader, whether in the church, military, business, politics, sports, or any context, to see if we can come up a personification of the ideal leader. More often than not, among qualities like "charisma," "organizational skills," and such the class members will include "commitment to Christ" or something to that effect in the list of qualities, but when we are done brainstorming, I will remove "commitment to Christ" and similar qualities, leaving a still very solid list of admirable leadership qualities. At that point, I show them a picture of who embodies those qualities that are left – Adolph Hitler. No kidding. Come up with just about any attribute of leadership and you can somehow attribute Hitler with having that quality – organizational skills, vision, commitment, ability to motivate. Amazingly, he even gave speeches which sounded almost as Christian as you would hear from a church leader today! My point in this exercise is not that we should emulate Hitler's leadership – to the contrary! – but that no leadership quality is a substitute for seeking first the Kingdom of God and his righteousness. Without that, even the most talented leader can become a monster.

This means that one's intimacy with God must be strongly guarded, lest a leader lose his character. Borek, Lovett and Towns wrote, "Those who are flawed morally may lack the character to avoid undermining their moral authority as leaders."[35] Pastor Bill Hybels was even more direct: "Every time you compromise character you compromise leadership."[36]

The character which results from intimacy with God must also be developed, especially since it is a universal trait to good leadership. "Character development is essential in every leadership style," write Borek, Lovett and Towns.[37] It is for this reason also that Paul wrote to Timothy that when choosing leaders of churches, he must choose one who is not a "recent convert" (1 Timothy 3:6) since the building of intimacy with God and the character which results from it takes time and effort. "Spiritual maturity," wrote Sanders, "is indispensable to good leadership. A novice or new convert should not be pushed into leadership."[38] Only those who have developed an intimacy with God demonstrated by character are qualified for leadership.

Perhaps not surprisingly, the world is longing for leaders who have this experience of inner transformation Paul speaks of in Romans 12 as the basis for their leadership, especially in the military. The world wants leaders who are leaders in their inmost being, not necessarily those who are in positions of leadership for a season and then cease leading, or those who can manage only to be in charge temporarily. People want to follow people who are leaders, not to follow people who lead; they want to follow those with innate leadership qualities. Captain W. Brad Johnson, USN (Ret), and Dr. Gregory P. Harper, instructors of leadership at the US Naval Academy, write of this innate leadership,

> What are the virtues upon which this approach to moral leadership is based? At USNA, we think of moral virtues as the internal composition of one's character. These are distinctly good and admirable human qualities that denote moral excellence or uprightness in the way one lives…The question we want midshipmen to ask themselves when decisions must be made is this: "What shall I be?" That is, what sort of agent or leader will I be? Not simply "What shall I do?" Although the second question must be answered day-to-day, the first question is more basic, more foundational, and more critical to ensuring excellent moral leadership among young officers we generate for the fleet.[39]

Clearly the US Navy desires officers who are leaders from the inside out, not those who are susceptible to external pressures or constantly changing ways of thinking. Clearly, whether they realize it or not, they want a Romans 12 type of leader.

Perhaps not so amazingly, so does the Army. The US Army's Leader to Leader Institute states,

> Many people naively think that leadership is a matter of a set of skills that the leader uses on other people: how to influence others, how to inspire others, how to rally others to a cause. But in our experience, and the Army's, leadership does not start with focusing on others; it starts with focusing on oneself. John P. Kotter, an award-winning expert on leadership at the Harvard Business School and the author of Leading Change and What Leaders Really Do, says, "I suspect a lot of people

just haven't been taught: always start with yourself. It is the great rule of thumb for so many things. Start with yourself first! And then go out from there. Don't try to teach mathematics until you've learned it yourself"...Leadership is a matter of how to be, not how to do it. Only a person who is comfortable in his or her own skin, who has a strong set of values, who behaves consistently with those values, who demonstrates self-discipline, can begin to lead others. Recognizing this truth, the Army's approach to leadership development focuses squarely on personal development and personal values, on character.[40]

Both the US Army and US Navy recognize the need for an internal drive to leadership, one grounded not on personal gain or selfish motives but on a clear understanding of right and wrong. The foundation for this is character, and whether they realize it or not, the ideal they are calling for the same inner foundational change that Paul is calling for in Romans 12. An intimacy with God – a dedication to Godliness coupled with a transformation of the mind – is the ultimate foundation for leadership. "Leadership is a matter of how to be, not how to do."[41]

Scripture is full of examples of spiritual intimacy being the foundation for leadership. In both a political and military setting, Joshua is a prime example. God's commission to him as the leader of His people gives an excellent indication of what God expects of all leaders. Joshua 1: 7-8 is a portion of God's commissioning statement and he tells Joshua,

Be strong and very courageous. Be careful to obey all the law my servant Moses gave you; do not turn from it to the right or to the left, that you may be successful wherever you go. Do not let this Book of the Law depart from your mouth; meditate on it day and night so that you may be careful to do everything written in it. Then you will be prosperous and successful.[42]

There is a definite "if...then" construction in God's charge to Joshua. Prosperity and success were both conditioned on the closeness Joshua maintained with God. Borek, Lovett, and Towns explain,

First, Joshua recognized the key to his success...would be tied to the discipline of meditating on the Word of God. The promise God gave him was tied to that responsibility. 'This book of the law shall not depart from your mouth, but you shall meditate in it day and night, that you may observe to do according to all that is written in it. For *then* you will make

your way prosperous, *and then* you will have good success'
(Joshua 1:8).[43] (Italics mine)

This has important implications for Joshua, specifically as a leader. As
Pickering stated:

> Joshua is challenged to perpetual faithfulness to the covenant.
> The preeminent duty of the ideal leader is to exemplify perfect
> obedience to the covenant demands of the law. He is to be
> 'strong and courageous,' a recurrent covenant challenge…The
> covenant law is to colour the leader's speech, fill his mind,
> and govern his entire life, thus producing prosperity. The
> ideal leader can be strong, brave, and unafraid because God
> is always with him. Normally, God's presence with the leader
> also implies his presence with the people.[44]

Joshua later demonstrated how he understood the level of commitment
required to be a successful leaders in God's sight. Before his first military
engagement as commander-in-chief without Moses' guidance, he ensures
he himself as well as his army are consecrated to God. Borek, Lovett, and
Towns explain, "Joshua understood he needed to be completely separated
to God if he expected the blessing of God. Before taking on the enemy,
Joshua called on the men of Israel to be circumcised at Gilgal."[45] This
circumcision was no mere rite of passage or religious ceremony; rather, as
Matthew Henry comments,

> God would by this teach them, and us with them, in all great
> undertakings to begin with God, to make sure of his favour,
> by offering ourselves to him as a living sacrifice.[46]

Joshua's example shows us how leadership, for any great endeavor
to which God calls us, must be founded on a personal dedication and
commitment to knowing and submitting ourselves to God.

Another example of intimacy with God as a prerequisite for leadership
is that of David. 1 Samuel 16:7 shows clearly what God looks for in a
potential leader as He sifted through potential candidates for the one who
would lead Israel as king and as commander. Interestingly, God did not
choose expertise, training, education, or physical prowess as essentials for
a leader who would take on this monumental task; he looked for only one
quality:

> But the Lord said to Samuel, "Do not consider his appearance
> or his height, for I have rejected him. The Lord does not look

at things man looks at. Man looks at the outward appearance, but the Lord looks at the heart."[47]

Put simply, while David was growing he could have spent his time in preparation for kingship and generalship (had he known what was in his future) by studying and practicing the arts of politics and warfare. These traits, however, in the eyes of the one who sovereignly chose David as king, were irrelevant. David had focused on the trait which God looks for most in potential leaders. "David qualified as a candidate for leadership by developing a heart for God."[48]

Gene Getz described what this "heart for God" is like:

> When God looked at David that day he was anointed king, He saw a man after His own heart – a man who understood who He really is. David was deeply affected by the reality of God's omnipotence, His omniscience, His omnipresence, His loving-kindness, faithfulness and righteousness…the Lord saw a man with a believing heart, a thankful heart, a truthful heart, an open heart, an expectant heart, a heart that cherished God's law, a sorrowful heart, a humble and dependant heart. That is why God chose David to be the future king of Israel.[49]

Amazingly, God looks for the intimacy of spirit far more than any other trait. It is far more important in God's eyes than training, education, practice, or even natural talent. God desires intimacy with him as a prerequisite for leadership, and if David is any indication, this intimacy begins long before God formally calls his leaders to leadership. As Oswald Sanders wrote,

> Often truly authoritative leadership falls on someone who years earlier sought to practice the discipline of seeking first the kingdom of God. Then as a person matures, God confers a leadership role, and the Spirit of God goes to work through him.[50]

When David yielded his throne to his son, Solomon, he highlighted this need for spiritual intimacy as he passed on his final words of advice. 1 Kings 2:1-4 records David's passing words to Solomon, and of any advice he could have passed to his son – whether in political shrewdness, setting visions and goals, learning the art of war, or whatever else – he says simply,

> Be strong, and show yourself a man, and observe what the

Lord your God requires: Walk in his ways, and keep his decrees and commands, his laws and requirements, as written in the Law of Moses, so that you may prosper in all you do and wherever you go.

In David and Solomon's day, a dynasty on the throne was the surest sign of success; coups against unsuccessful leaders were common and well noted in the Old Testament. God promised David that as long as he and his sons walked in his ways he would guarantee their success, signified perpetually by a descendant on the throne. David explained to Solomon that certainly a leader is to be strong and "be a man," or set the example of manly virtues, but the essence of doing so is to know God, know what he wants, and dedicate oneself to doing it. When a leader does so, God is faithful to support and guide that person as a leader and bring about success, and this is far more important in God's sight than any other leadership attribute. Matthew Henry stated,

> Let each, in his own age, successively, observe what God requires, and then God will be sure to keep his promise. We never let fall the promise until we let fall the precept. God had promised David that the Messiah would come from his descendants, and that promise was absolute: But that promise that there should not fail to be a man on the throne of Israel was conditional – if his descendants behave themselves, as they should. If Solomon, in his day, fulfills the condition, he does his part towards the perpetuating of the promise. The condition is that he walk before God in all his policies, in sincerity, with zeal and resolution.[51]

A leader will gain the fulfillment of God's calling if, and only if, he dedicates himself to knowing God and following him closely.

Later, God reemphasizes the same point after Solomon's stages a remarkable public display of his and his nation's devotion to God through the dedication of the new Temple. In a dream, God says to Solomon,

> As for you, if you walk before me as your father David walked, and you do according to all that I have commanded you, and if you keep My statutes and My judgments, then I will establish your kingdom, as I covenanted with David your father, saying, "You shall not fail to have a man as ruler in Israel." But if you turn away and forsake My statutes and My commandments which I have set before you, and go and serve

other gods, and worship them, then I will uproot them from My land which I have given them; and this house which I have sanctified for My name I will cast out of my sight, and will make it a proverb and a byword among all peoples. (2 Chronicles 7: 17-20, NKJV)[52]

Once again, the Scripture is clear that success for a leader called by God is dependent upon that leader's dedication to knowing and following God, being "pure in heart and action, living the life I've set out for you, attentively obedient to my guidance and judgments"[53] as Peterson paraphrased. As Pickering wrote, "The promises of the Davidic Covenant are also reaffirmed. But, these promises depend upon obedience to God's law. David's dynasty will never lack for an heir. However, unfaithfulness will bring humiliation and shame…"[54] It is to be one extreme or another – either tremendous blessing and success, or certain failure.

And again, the Scripture shows us how a leader called by God is told clearly that walking closely with him is a prerequisite to the certainty of receiving his blessings. In 2 Chronicles 15: 1-7, God reminds Asa of his duties to Him after Asa experienced a great success.

Now the Spirit of God came upon Azariah the son of Oded. And he went out to meet Asa, and said to him: "Hear me Asa, and all Judah and Benjamin. The Lord is with you while you are with him. If you seek Him, He will be found by you; but if you forsake him, He will forsake you. For a long time Israel has been without a true God, without a teaching priest, and without law; but when in their trouble they turned to the Lord God of Israel, and sought Him, He was found by them. And in those times there was no peace to the one who went out, nor to the one who came in, but great turmoil was on all the inhabitants of the lands. So nation was destroyed by nation, and city by city, for God troubled them with every adversity. But you, be strong and do not let your hands be weak, for your work shall be rewarded."[55]

Good times come and go through the life of any leader, but God calls the leader first and foremost, regardless of whether the times are prosperous or lean, to commit himself to God and follow Him. Matthew Henry explained,

"Here was a prophet sent to Asa and his army, when they returned victorious from the war with the Cushites, not to

18

congratulate them on their success but to quicken them to their duty…He told them very plainly on what terms they stood with God. Let them not think that, having obtained this victory, all was their own forever. Let them do well, and it will be well with them, otherwise not."[56]

God wished to remind Asa that ultimately the success was His to give and that he would only give it to Asa as king if Asa walked with God. "God's attitude toward his people," wrote Barton and Muddiman, "corresponds with their attitude toward Him."[57] The blessings of God were completely conditional on the king's closeness to God. Asa, then, had no inherent skill that would guarantee success for himself and for his people; he, as does any leader, needed to commit himself to a closeness with God which would allow him to know that to which God called him.

An example of this devotion and the results of it was King Jehoshaphat, as recorded in 2 Chronicles 17:

> Now the Lord was with Jehoshaphat, because he walked in the former ways of his father David; he did not seek the Baals, but sought the God of his father, and walked in His commandments and not according to the acts of Israel. Therefore the LORD established the kingdom in his hand; and all Judah gave presents to Jehoshaphat, and he had riches and honor in abundance. And his heart took delight in the ways of the Lord; moreover he removed the high places and wooden images from Judah…And the fear of the Lord fell on all the kingdoms of the lands that were around Judah, so that they did not make war against Jehoshaphat…So Jehoshaphat became increasingly powerful.[58]

The chronicler makes it very clear that God was with Jehoshaphat because he walked with God, not because of his ability as a strategic planner, his intelligence, his resourcefulness, or his business savvy. He was successful for one simple reason – he walked with God, or as Peterson stated it, Jehoshaphat was "single minded in following God" (*The Message*).[59] Matthew Henry gives insight as well into the nature of this walk – Jehoshaphat did not follow out of religious obligation or begrudgingly or even as a matter of "filling squares", but "he was lively and affectionate in his religion…cheerful and pleasant with it; he went on in his work with alacrity."[60] Jehoshaphat showed a happy passion – a wholehearted desire, a delight – to know God and follow him, and the results were very noticeable. He had honor, riches, and power, all results of his desire to wholeheartedly follow God.

Evidence that the blessing of God on one of His leaders is conditional upon the dedication shown by that leader is the life of King Uzziah in 2 Chronicles 26: 4-5, which states, "[Uzziah] did what was right in the days of Zechariah, who had understanding in the visions of God; and as long as he sought the Lord, God made him prosper."[61] God blessed Uzziah as a military commander, as an administrator, in securing his kingdom, and in many other ways. Yet, he lost his intimacy with God: "His fame spread far and wide, for he was greatly helped until he became powerful. But after Uzziah became powerful, his pride led to his downfall. He was unfaithful to the Lord his God" (vs. 15-16).[62] Clearly as long as Uzziah remained faithful to God and pursued an intimacy with Him, Uzziah was successful as king; when his pride took the place of the desire to know and follow God, Uzziah failed. "Uzziah's long reign and successes are regarded as a result of seeking God," commented Barton and Muddiman. "The same logic dictates that Uzziah's illness was caused by a previous falling… Thus, like some kings before him, Uzziah's reign falls into two periods: one positive and one negative."[63] The chronicler shows a clear cause and effect action in Uzziah's case – a desire for intimacy with God led to successful leadership; the loss of it led to failure.

The chronicler gives other examples of the success of Judah's kings being conditioned on the dedication the king had to following the Lord. 2 Chronicles 27:6 states, "So Jotham became mighty, *because* [emphasis mine] he prepared his way before the Lord his God."[64] Again, clearly, Jotham's might was due to his dedication to God and to that only, not for any other reason – it was "rooted in his steady and determined life of obedience to God" (*The Message*).[65] Likewise, Hezekiah found success because of his intimacy with God. 2 Chronicles 31: 20-21 states,

> Thus Hezekiah did throughout all Judah, and he did what was good and right and true before the Lord his God. And in every work that he began in the service of the house of God, in the law and in the commandment, to seek his God, he did it with all his heart. So he prospered."[66]

Like Jehoshaphat, Hezekiah showed a passion for following God. In every work, he sought God and he did so with his entire heart. The result was that he prospered as a leader.

For every spiritual gift, then, and especially so for the gift and calling of leadership, God demands of his people an intimacy with Him as top priority. As often as a leader can work on and enhance other leadership attributes, he will not ultimately succeed without a relationship with God that allows him to understand God and know what He requires. On the other hand, when a leader has and maintains that intimacy, there is no limit to the impact he can have; he can accomplish all things to which God calls him. The bottom line for all leaders is found in Micah 6:6-8, where Micah says, "He has shown you, oh man, what is good, and what does the Lord require of you but to do justly, to love mercy, and to walk humbly with your God." God calls each of us, especially leaders to a close walk with Him. As Matthew Henry wrote,

> We must, in the whole course of our conduct, conform ourselves to the will of God, maintain our communion with God, and study to approve ourselves to him…That is what God requires, and without which the most costly services are meaningless offerings.[67]

As good as a leader has the potential for being, he can ultimately do nothing without that closeness with God.

Paul D. Cairney

CHAPTER 3.
How Leaders Can Gain Spiritual Intimacy

Becoming intimate with God takes deliberate action on the part of the leader – and even the future leader who does not even know he will be a leader, as in David's case – and Scriptures gives some insight as to how to achieve the intimacy God requires of a leader.

The first means by which one may become intimate with God is through communication. Communication with God comes through two means: God communicating with us through His revealed word, and a mutual communication through prayer.

When Joshua received his call to lead the nation of Israel, God told him specifically that he was to "meditate on [the law] day and night"[68] (Joshua 1:8 NIV). Peterson's paraphrase is even more emphatic: "And don't for a minute let this Book of the Revelation be out of your mind. Ponder and meditate on it day and night (*The Message*)."[69] God expects his followers to be forever thinking on and internalizing his message; it is not simply memorization, but a conscious attempt to know and understand what God's word means and how to apply it. It is more than knowing what it says, but actually pondering what it means. This is critical to a leader called by God. Matthew Henry stated, "If ever any man's business might have excused him from meditation, and other acts of devotion, one would think Joshua's might at this time…and yet he must find time and thoughts for meditation."[70] A leader, by the very nature of the work, is a busy person and yet he must make this the top priority in his life. No man or woman can dare claim to be a leader called by God who ignores the very word of God or treats it casually. "We also must give ourselves to the study of the Scriptures," wrote Charles Stanley. "The Bible reveals who God is and what he has done. If we really want to know him, we will set aside time to partake of the living Word, letting His divine counsel saturate our minds."[71] The leader called by God must make the time to search God's word for understanding of who God is. This is hardly a sacrifice, however; no leader can fail to be blessed who does so.

Likewise, a leader chosen by God must remain in contact with God in order to fulfill God's calling. This must also do by prayer. Again, this cannot be casual, but consciously done. Sanders wrote, "The spiritual leader should outpace the rest of the [organization], above all, in prayer."[72] Certainly this must be true; if God chooses a person through whom God wishes to influence others, must not that person be the first to ask of God and desire to discern his thoughts? Stanley wrote,

> Hearing the Scriptures on Sunday morning or through other means is helpful, but there is no substitute for spending time alone with the Savior. Spiritual intimacy requires quiet moments when God can speak clearly to your heart and when you can speak honestly to Him. We need to spend time alone win prayer, meditation, and worship of Christ. We come to hear from Him, not just receive from Him. We come to adore Him, praise, Him and delight in Him.[73]

Logically we see this, and through example we see it as well. As E.M. Bounds pointed out,

Great leaders of the Bible were great at prayer. They weren't leaders because of brilliancy of thought, because they were exhaustless in resources, because of their magnificent culture or native endowment, but because, by the power of prayer, they could command the power of God."[74]

Great leaders called by God become great because of their ability to pray, to the exclusion of all else. For all a leader's strengths and assets, he is nothing without dedicating himself to prayer and seeking God. Likewise, a leader may have significant shortcomings, yet he may overcome them through prayer and communication with God.

This communication with God is by no means a sacrifice; in fact it is the best thing a leader can do. Charles Haddon Spurgeon, a great preacher and church leader, said it simply: "The most needful and profitable labour is that which we spend on our own mental and spiritual improvement."[75] Towns, Borek, and Lovett echo that thought: "Time alone with God is the best investment leaders can make with their time. Joshua learned that lesson from the example of Moses and began practicing that discipline in his own life."[76] Indeed, through logic and example we can see how those who are called by God to leadership must make the time to spend with God in knowing His word and in prayer.

As an interesting military application, Navy Captain James Stockdale, a senior ranking prisoner of war in the infamous Hanoi Hilton in Viet Nam established several rules for all prisoners to follow. Listed among the top four was, simply, to pray.[77] Especially in such a strenuous environment, prayer was essential and the leaders knew they needed it to survive and win.

The second means for a leader to find intimacy with God is to not only know but to accept God's standards. This means that the leader must "conform himself in every thing to the law of God, and make this his rule."[78] In other words, a leader must do more than just know what God's standards are, but to make God's standards one's own – to mirror God's ways in one's one life. Solomon wrote in Proverbs 3: 5 that one should "Trust in the Lord with all your heart and lean not on your own understanding; in all your ways acknowledge Him and He will make your paths straight"[79] (NIV). One must adopt the Lord's mindset if one is to truly be intimate with Him and to be effective as a leader. Once we do so, we must then do what God says. James wrote,

> Do not merely listen to the word, and so deceive yourselves. Do what it says. Anyone who listens to the word but does not do what it says is like a man who looks at his face in a mirror and, after looking at himself, goes away and immediately forgets what he looks like. But the man who looks intently into the perfect law that gives freedom, and continues to do this, not forgetting what he has heard, but doing it – he will be blessed in what he does.[80] (1:22-25)

One might think that wholehearted obedience is more a byproduct of intimacy with God instead of what makes intimacy, and yet a sure way to compromise one's intimacy with God is to not wholeheartedly follow his word.

This bedrock of belief on which action is then built is essential for a leader. Kouzes and Posner point out the need for understanding what we believe:

> Values inform us of what to do and what not to do. They are the guiding principles in our lives with respect to the personal and social ends we desire – such as salvation and peace – and with respect to moral conduct and personal ompetence – such as honest and imagination.[81]

For a Christian, this means to value what God values and to act

25

accordingly. Without such core beliefs, a leader will be ineffective and perhaps even dangerous.

To be credible as a leader, you must first clarify your own values, the standards by which you choose to live your life. Values guide how you feel, what you say, what you think, how you make choices and how you act...Without core beliefs and with only shifting positions, would-be leaders will be judged as inconsistent and will be derided for being 'political' in their behavior.[82]

> The Real Goal
>
> One question I had to ask myself as a leader was weather God was truly my top priority or if I was using him as a means to reach my own personal ambitions. It is true that God wants us to succeed, but his real desire is that we seek him first. I had to ask myself this question: "If God never blessed my leadership again, would I still seek him?" The answer needs to be yes, and if it is not then my priorities are backward. Otherwise, I am using God merely as a means to get what I want.

Another essential aspect to gain intimacy with God is submission to God. This means that the would-be leader must place God first in all things. Again, using Joshua's reception of his commission from God as an example, we see that fully obeying God's word is essential for a leader. Peterson paraphrased it as such: "Give it everything you have, heart and soul. Make sure you carry out the Revelation that Moses commanded you, *every bit of it*" [emphasis mine] (*The Message*).[83] Expanding on this, Matthew Henry wrote,

> He [Joshua] must be careful to obey all the law. Joshua was a man of great power and authority, yet he must himself be under command and do as he is bidden. No man's dignity or dominion, however great, sets him above the law of God.[84]

Often, this requirement runs counter to the natural impulse of a leader to be preeminent. Leaders are frequently those who enjoy the status and singularity of being the one in charge, and yet God calls us to ensure we follow him first if we desire to lead. As Larry Michael wrote, "A Christian leader must first be led by God before he can lead others."[85] He later points out that this is not only necessary, but it is the most important thing: "We make it our goal to please him (2 Corinthians 5:9, NIV). That goal becomes the all-encompassing aim of every Christian leader."[86] Towns, Lovett, and Borek agree that this is essential, and that it will positively impact one's ability to lead. "Ultimately, growing leaders need to nurture their relationship with God. As they learn to become good followers of Christ, they become better leaders."[87]

This is no simple task for potential leaders to attain, nor for veteran leaders to maintain. J. Oswald Sanders made the point that,

> God wants to show such people how strong He really is. But not all who aspire to leadership are willing to pay such a high personal price. Yet there is no compromise here: In the secret reaches of the heart this price is paid, before any public office or honor. Our Lord made it clear to James and John that high position in the kingdom of God is reserved for those whose hearts –even the secret places where no one else probes—are qualified. God's sovereign searching of our hearts, and then His call to leadership, are awesome to behold. And they make a person very humble.[88]

Humility before God and putting Him first is the price that must be paid for effective leadership. Part of putting God first is putting one and one's personal interests in a secondary place. Humility is the sign that a leader has placed God first, and God will not bless that leader until that humility is in place. Henry and Mel Blackaby stated,

> Now I want you to know that God is using men and women of great talent and ability. But when He does, the first assignment of the Holy Spirit is to bring humility. They must cease to compare themselves to others and measure themselves against Almighty God. The Holy Spirit must deal with their self-image and replace it with the image of Christ. This is not an easy task.[89]

A leader must submit himself fully and without reservation before he can claim an intimacy with God, and therefore be effective as a leader. According to Spurgeon, God would not even partly be used of God until this submission was fully in place; he "believed that one could not be used of God until self-confidence was depleted."[90] Submission to God is not an option.

Nor is it an easy or enjoyable task. Samuel Brengle of the Salvation Army counted the cost that a person must make in self-interest before God could use him as a leader.

> It is not won by promotion, but my many prayers and tears. It

is attained by confession of sin, and much heartsearching and humbling before God; by self-surrender, a courageous sacrifice of every idol, a bold uncomplaining embrace of the cross, and by an eternal, unfaltering looking unto Jesus crucified. It is not gained by seeking great things for ourselves, but like Paul, by counting those things that are gain to us as a loss for Christ. This the a great price, but it must be paid by the leader who would not be merely a nominal but a real spiritual leader of men, a leader whose power is recognized and felt in heaven, on earth, and in hell.[91]

There is a high price to be paid for one to fully submit himself to God which will allow the intimacy with God necessary for one to be a leader. Yet this is what is required.

To find the intimacy with God which makes a leader, a person must consciously seek to know God through meditation on Scripture and through prayer, must make God's values one's very own and live by them, and must humble himself and keep God as his top priority. Then and only then will a person find that intimacy with God. As the Richard and Henry Blackaby wrote, "Spiritual leadership flows out of a person's vibrant, intimate relationship with God. You cannot be a spiritual leader if you are not meeting God in profound, life-changing ways."[92] Stanley sums it up perfectly – "There is no substitute for personal intimacy with God. Nothing compares to it – it is the key to everything."[93]

PART II
Leadership as the Gift of the Holy Spirit

Henry and Richard Blackaby cite a recent survey by George Barna which is both enlightening and disturbing about the knowledge and understanding of the spiritual gift of leadership. The survey asked senior pastors from many denominations whether or not they had the spiritual gift of leadership. The results were stunning. As the Blackabys reported,

> When asked if they believed they had the spiritual gift of leadership, only 6 percent responded yes! The fact that 94 percent of the senior pastors surveyed did not believe they were gifted to be leaders may explain the sense of desperation many church leaders express as they examine their ministry and its current effectiveness.[94]

Assuming these pastors were giving honest answers and not attempting to sound modest, we can draw one of two conclusions from this survey: We can either conclude that God has called numerous members to leadership within His church and has equipped only about one in twenty to carry out that mission, or we can conclude that many of these senior pastors do not understand what the gift of leadership really is. Both answers would certainly lead to the desperation the Blackabys sense in church leaders.

By looking closer at what Scripture says about the gift of leadership, however, we can understand the frequently misunderstood difference between gifts and talents in general, as well as the application and acquisition of gifts in general and leadership in particular, and see how they can be applied to the military setting.

CHAPTER 4
Defining Spiritual Gifts

The term "gift" in current English usually means one of two things. It either means a present, an item given by one person to another free of charge and free of conditions, or it means an exceptional talent that one person possesses which stands out in comparison to other people. While to an extent accurate, neither of these common uses satisfies as a definition when applied to spiritual gifts. Spiritual gifts are indeed freely given, but they are by no means given without any conditions. In fact, the opposite is true; God gives these gifts with a specific purpose. Matthew Henry adamantly stated in his commentary that "whatever gifts God confers on any man, he confers them that he may do good with them. They are not given for show, but for service."[95] Gifts are abilities God gives his people that they may serve Him in the way He desires. Additionally, while "gifts" and "talents" may both mean extraordinary abilities, to use the terms synonymously is to misunderstand the real concept of spiritual gifts and the purpose for why God has given them.

The most useful and clear definition of spiritual gifts comes from the twelfth chapter of Paul's first letter to the Corinthians, where he states,

> There are different kinds of gifts, but the same Spirit. There are different kinds of service, but the same Lord. There are different kinds of working, but the same God works all of them in all men. Now to each one is given the manifestation of the Spirit for the common good...All these are the work of one and the same Spirit, and he gives them to each one, just as he determines (1 Corinthians 12:4-7,11, NIV).[96]

Using this passage as a foundation, D.A. Carson defines spiritual gifts simply: "Spiritual gifts [are] the full range of the manifestations of the Spirit."[97] The key word here and in this passage is "manifestation," the same word used in this passage in the New International Version, the New

King James Version, Darby's Translation, and a host of other translations. This applies not only to the passage in 1 Corinthians, but also to other references to gifts: As Billy Graham wrote,

> The word *charismata* is the plural of *charisma* and, except for one passage in 1 Peter, is found only in the writings of the apostle Paul. If we define it precisely, it means 'manifestation of grace,' and is translated "gifts." [98]

The American Heritage Dictionary of the English Language defines "manifestation" as "an indication of the existence, reality or presence of something" and "one of the forms in which someone or something, such as a person, a divine being, or an idea, is revealed."[99] This means that spiritual gifts (*charismata*) are God being revealed.

Paul states in 1 Corinthians 12 that the Holy Spirit is the giver of these abilities. D.A. Carson states that these abilities "manifest the Spirit; they show the Spirit"[100]; Eugene Peterson's translation, *The Message*, says they "show who God is"[101]; the Amplified Bible is, "the evidence, the spiritual illumination of the Spirit."[102] All of these, therefore, lead us to conclude that a spiritual gift is an ability given by the Holy Spirit through which the Holy Spirit can manifest himself, or stated another way, spiritual gifts are abilities given by the Holy Spirit to a believer through which the Holy Spirit will reveal His presence or show Himself.

This working definition of spiritual gifts helps to clarify much of the confusion about the gifts and their use. It can especially clarify the distinction between spiritual gifts and talents. Both certainly are enhanced or even extraordinary abilities, yet the difference is simply where the Holy Spirit in his sovereignty chooses to manifest himself. When we see it in this light, we are more likely to understand the functions of gifts as opposed to talents because gifts are the Holy Spirit's manifestation of himself. In speaking of gifts, the Blackabys point out, "The question we ask is self-centered: 'What can I do for God?' The question we should be asking is God-centered: 'What does God want to do through me? What is his particular assignment for me?'"[103] Spiritual gifts are God's way of working that "particular assignment" through each believer. Talents are not God's chosen way of working a "particular assignment."

Does this imply that talents do not glorify God? The answer to that is clearly no. We can, and should, use our gifts to glorify God. As Bruce Bugbee, author of *What You Do Best in the Body of Christ*, rightly said, "Although natural talents and spiritual gifts are not the same, all that we have ought to and can be used to glorify God and edify others."[104] Likewise, as Paul wrote to the Colossians, "Whatever you do, in word or deed, do it all in the name of the Lord Jesus, giving thanks to God the Father through him" (Colossians 3:17, NIV).[105] Nor do spiritual gifts negate the importance of talents. As Oswald Sanders pointed out,

> The coming of spiritual gifts in the life of the Christian does not eliminate natural gifts, but enhances and stimulates them. New birth in Christ does not change natural qualities, but when they are placed under the control of the Holy Spirit, they are raised to new effectiveness. Hidden abilities are often released.[106]

We can also deduce, then, that natural talents may actually become spiritual gifts. In other words, the Holy Spirit may choose to transform a talent into the means by which he glorifies himself. This is not done by our own choosing, but by that of the Holy Spirit. As Bugbee stated, "Natural talents may be transformed *by the Holy Spirit* and empowered as spiritual gifts" [emphasis mine].[107]

Sanders also points out that spiritual gifts and talents need not operate exclusively of each other. In speaking of leadership in particular, he says it is quite to the contrary:

Spiritual leadership blends natural and spiritual qualities. Yet even natural qualities are supernatural gifts, since all good things come from God...Both natural and spiritual qualities reach their greatest effectiveness when employed in the service of God and for His glory.[108]

So, in short, the difference between spiritual gifts and talents can be summarized as such: Spiritual gifts are abilities given to us by the Holy Spirit through which the Holy Spirit chooses to glorify himself; talents are abilities which we possess through genetics or other inherent sources through which we can choose to glorify God or not.

So how can these senior pastors, or any leader, tell if they have the gift of leadership as opposed to just a talent for leadership? One can tell, simply speaking, by analyzing one's process of leadership, by analyzing the results of one's leadership, and by analyzing the source of one's leadership. To know if the Holy Spirit is in our process of leadership, we should ask ourselves as the Blackabys ask, "Do you make your decisions based upon your ability to achieve the results, or upon the Spirit's leading and equipping?"[109] In other words, if we involve God fully in our leadership, he is faithful to personally guide us to where he desires us to be. Then we must determine, as Charles Haddon Spurgeon stated, if the Holy Spirit is in the results. "On the whole," he wrote, "experience is our surest test, and if God upholds us from year to year, and gives us his blessing, we need make no other trial of our vocation."[110] Finally, as the Blackabys point out, "There is a…goal leaders should have for their organizations, one which is the ultimate goal of any organization…to bring God glory…[T]heir goal ought to be to glorify God by the way they lead their organization."[111] All three elements are essential in this though. If we seek God but ultimately don't see the results, then it may be that we are not actually heeding his calling and perhaps putting our agendas ahead of his. On the other hand, if we are seeing positive results without consulting the Holy Spirit then we may be achieving goals apart from what the Holy Spirit has in mind, or we are confusing blessings with luck which will no doubt soon run out. Finally, remembering that a spiritual gift is the Holy Spirit showing himself through his people, if the Holy Spirit does not receive the glory in one's leadership then he is not manifesting himself and therefore one does not have the spiritual gift of leadership however talented one may be in it.

Using this distinction between spiritual gifts and talents, especially the third element of it, yields another benefit: When we realize that the Holy Spirit is choosing to reveal himself through us – that it is of his actions and not of our own – we are less likely to be become arrogant or inflated as we see their effectiveness. The realization of God's sovereignty will negate our own pride. The effects are truly not our own, and we dare not take any credit for them or for the results we see. As Paul wrote to the Corinthians, "But one and the same Spirit works all these things, distributing to each one individually *as He wills*" (I Cor 12: 11, NKJV) [emphasis mine].[112] Billy Graham, too, stated, "These gifts come to us from the Holy Spirit. *He chooses* [emphasis mine] who gets which gifts, and He dispenses them at His good pleasure."[113]

And yet another benefit to this clarification is that we gain a greater confidence in the use of spiritual gifts because we know that it is the Holy Spirit who is manifesting himself through us, and he will certainly not fail. What Larry Michael wrote about the gift of leadership is also applicable to any spiritual gift,

> More than anything else, as Christians, we have the confidence of the leadership of the Holy Spirit as we implement different approaches to leading. As we are sensitive to the Spirit's leading, we can…have confidence that the Lord will lead us in the right direction.[114]

CHAPTER 5
Spiritual Gifts Applied
Beyond The Church Context

Before we seek to apply the gift of leadership or any spiritual gift to the military, we need to know if we even can apply spiritual gifts beyond—not exclusive of but in addition to—the church context. In other words, is the gift of leadership limited to deacons, elders, senior pastors, or Sunday School coordinators, or can the gift of leadership be applied to the military, business, politics, or any other secular activity? Certainly the immediate application for Paul's instructions on spiritual gifts is within the local churches to which he wrote, and Grudem's definition of spiritual gifts as "any ability that is empowered by the Holy Spirit and used in any ministry in the church"[115] is no doubt true, but is there an automatic restriction to the applications of spiritual gifts to the immediate church context? Can one use the gift of leadership, or any gift, in education, in athletics, or any other non-ministerial fashion?

To an extent, the answer to this question is an argument from silence. While there is nothing which explicitly says how to use a spiritual gift beyond of the church context, neither is there any prohibition of it. As Carson wrote about the gift of leadership,

> The second word (*kyberneseis*) is primarily used for the piloting or steering of a ship; its use is metaphorical here. Some have suggested that these two gifts represent the spiritual enduement necessary for the offices of deacon and bishop respectively. Doubtless that much is true; but there is nothing to suggest that these gifts are restricted to people serving in these offices.[116]

If there is no explicit prohibition to using spiritual gifts outside the church, then logic also tells us that there are some, if not all, spiritual gifts which must be used in places other than the immediate church context. For instance, if we consider the gift of evangelism (Ephesians 4:11) and state that this gift as well as any gift must only be used within the community of believers, then the evangelist is almost literally preaching to the choir. Evangelism is far less effective if it is only exercised within the church; indeed the evangelist must leave the confines of the church to fully exercise his gift. Likewise, Paul says that the gift of tongues is a sign "not to those who believe, but to unbelievers" (I Corinthians 14: 22)[117] so clearly the intended beneficiaries of this gift is not the community of believers but those outside the community; in other words it must not be confined to the church context.

Indeed, there seems to be a false indication that spiritual gifts in general and leadership in particular can only be used within the confines of the local church, and if the senior pastors in the Barna survey are correct then the gifts are not being used there either. But numerous scholars refute this idea. Henry and Richard Blackaby, for example, argue that this is a false restriction to the use of gifts.

> People tend to draw distinctions between secular and spiritual matters. God is not restrained by such artificial boundaries. He is as powerful in the business world as he is in the church. God's wisdom applies as much to mergers, or investments, or hiring personnel, as it does to church matters. Decisions made in the political arena can have far-reaching ramifications and require prayer for God's guidance...God is pleased to direct people to choices that will bring him the greatest honor.[118]

They later say powerfully that this has been a common misperception throughout Biblical history:

> The problem was the Israelite's assumption that spiritual concerns, such as righteous living and obedience to God, belonged in the religious realm while the practical issues of doing battle with enemies, strengthening the economy, and unifying the country were secular matters. They forgot that God himself had won their military victories, brought them prosperity, and created their nation. He was as active on the battlefield as he was in the worship service. When the Israelites separated spiritual concerns from political and

> **A Gifted Leader**
> One of my favorite leaders is General Robert E. Lee. No doubt he was a talented leader, but could we also say he was a spiritually gifted leader? J. William Jones chronicled his time serving as Lee's chaplain in his book, *Christ in the Camp*, and wrote that, because of Lee's personal dedication to Christ, God used Lee as a catalyst for a spiritual revival in the Confederate Army – and what leader wouldn't want this in their organization? Some have argued that, since Lee ultimately lost the war he could not have possessed the spiritual gift of leadership, which can be a valid point. However, viewing Lee's leadership and influence in the context of his life and not just of the Civil War, you can point out that Lee probably had more influence than anyone in re-unifying the nation after the war by his example and attitude. If we look at it this way, realizing that as the heavens are higher than the earth God's ways are higher than our ways, and we can see that God's intended purpose for Lee's leadership went far beyond just his leadership on the battlefield, but for the spiritual growth of his soldiers and the re-birth of the United States.

economic issues, their nation was brought to its knees. Scripture indicates that it is a mistake to separate the spiritual from the secular world. Applying spiritual principles to business and political issues don't call for Baptist pastors to serve as military generals, nor does it require seminary professors to run the economy. God created people to be spiritual beings. Every person, Christian and non-Christian alike, is a spiritual person with spiritual needs. Employees, customers, and governing boards all have spiritual needs that God wants to meet through his servants in the workplace. God is also the author of human relationships. He has established laws in relationships that have not changed with the passing of time. To violate God-ordained relationship principles in the workplace is to invite disaster. Jesus Christ is the Lord of all believers whether they are at church or at work. The kingdom of God is, in fact, the rule of God in every area of life, including the church, home, workplace, and neighborhood. To ignore these truths when entering the business orld or political arena is to do so at one's peril.[119]

Charles Stanley firmly agreed with that sentiment. Referring to the gift of leadership as the gift of organization, he stated:

The person with the gift of organization is no less spiritual than those who bear any of the other ministry gifts. In fact, to the Christian all things are spiritual. There is no distinction before God between secular life and spiritual life – all of life is spiritual. Everything has a spiritual foundation.[120]

Rick Warren would certainly agree. "There are no unspiritual activities," he wrote, "only misused ones."[121]

Clearly, then, the Holy Spirit intends to manifest himself through his people in all aspects of life, not just within the context of the church. This should be a very liberating thought for those who do not find themselves called by God to an active ministry in the local church or even para-church ministry. As the Blackabys wrote, "The empowerment...is for every believer, not just those who are 'called into the ministry'."[122]

CHAPTER 6
A Word Of Caution: Balance Between Prideful And Strong Leadership

And while this is indeed a liberating thought, that the gift of leadership and any gift may be used either within or beyond the church context, we must also proceed with caution since the use of any spiritual gift, especially one as preeminent and visible as that of leadership, can quickly turn into a tool for selfish purposes. Perhaps this is why Paul prefaces his list of spiritual gifts in Romans 12 with the warning, "For I say, through the grace given to me, to everyone who is among you, not to think of himself more highly than he ought to think, but to think soberly, as God has dealt to each one a measure of faith" (Romans 12: 3, NKJV).[123] It is very easy to allow the idea of leadership, especially that of God-given leadership, to become license for selfish ambition. Sadly, there are numerous examples of this throughout Scripture, where effective and God-driven leaders chose selfish motives over following God.

One example is Saul. He was effective and powerful and won many battles, yet God ultimately deserted him. God's explanation of this to Samuel was quite simple, "I regret that I have set up Saul as king, for he has turned back from following me, and has not performed my commandments" (1 Samuel 15:10, NKJV).[124] Quite simply, God had his plans and had Saul in place as a leader to carry out those plans, and Saul chose to pursue his own goals rather than those God had intended. Saul evidently saw popularity and the admiration of the nation as a greater goal than following God's commandments, because he later confessed his transgression by stating, "I have sinned...because I feared the people and obeyed their voice" (1 Samuel 15: 24, NKJV).[125] The Blackabys make an excellent point about what it means to follow God's will instead of the will of the people the leader is supposed to lead:

> While it is true that leaders have motives, spiritual leaders are directed by the Holy Spirit, not by their own agendas… Spiritual leaders do not try to satisfy the goals and ambitions of the people they lead but those of the God whom they serve. Spiritual leaders must be spiritual statesmen and not spiritual politicians[126]

Sadly, Saul was not the only example. His successor, David, also allowed his authority as a leader to get in the way of his ability to do God's will. When he ordered a census of his people, the result was the death of seventy thousand men. Why was this? As Matthew Henry wrote,

Numbering the people, one would think, was no bad thing. Why should not the shepherd know the number of his flock? But God sees not as man sees. It is plain it was wrong in David to do it, and a great provocation to God, because he did it in the pride of his heart.[127]

But pride in what? It was pride in his strength as a leader and, presumably, in his desire for more of it. John Maxwell pointed out, "David's choice to count his soldiers revealed he was beginning to place more confidence in his troops than in the power of God."[128] Leadership in so many ways means the use of power and influence and when we realize that this power comes from God to use as he wishes we can keep ourselves in check. Yet when we start to see it as an inherent part of ourselves and forget that our leadership is God revealing himself through us, it can lead to disaster. "Never forget," wrote the Blackabys, "that the Spirit is given to each one to equip us to do God's will, not our will."[129] Millard Erikson would agree. "The gifts that we have," he wrote, "are bestowals upon us by the Holy Spirit. We should recognize that they are not our own accomplishments. They are intended to be used in the fulfillment of his plan."[130] To keep from falling as David did, leaders today would be wise to heed Richard Henry's words,

> Whatever we have that is good, God has given to us. The best and most useful man in the world is no more, no better, than what the free grace of God makes him every day. When we are thinking of ourselves, we must remember not to think of how much we have attained; but think how kind God has been to us…God gives his gifts in a certain measure: According to the measure of faith…Christ had the Spirit given him without measure. But the saints have it by measure. Christ, who had

gifts without measure, was meek and lowly; and shall we who are stinted be proud and self-conceited?[131]

Yet another example of how leadership can easily lead to abuse is that of Rehoboam, David's grandson. As he took the throne, a number of his subjects came to him to request that he reduce the many burdens Solomon had put on them. Rehoboam's elders agreed and said, "If you are kind to these people, and please them, and speak good words to them, they will be your servants forever" (2 Chronicles 10: 7, NKJV).[132] Instead he listened to his younger friends and took a more dictatorial approach:

> Then the king answered them roughly. King Rehoboam rejected the advice of the elders, and he spoke to them according to the advice of the young men, saying, 'My father made your yoke heavy, but I will add to it; my father chastised you with whips, but I will chastise you with scourges!' (2 Chronicles 10:13-14, NKJV)[133]

The result was open revolt which permanently divided the kingdom. When leaders deal harshly with those in their charge, they do so out of pride and perhaps a sense of superiority which is hardly becoming of a leader whose abilities are of the Holy Spirit. As Henry wrote,

> We must take heed of having too great an opinion of ourselves. We must not be self-conceited, nor esteem too much our own wisdom. There is a high thought of ourselves too good to be the slaves of sin and drudges to this world. We should think soberly, that is, we must have a modest option of ourselves and our own abilities, according to what we have received from God, and not otherwise.[134]

Henry also wrote, with no little sarcasm,

> God has given gifts to others as well as to ourselves. If we had the monopoly of the Spirit there might be some pretence for this conceitedness of ourselves; but others have their share as well as we. Therefore it ill becomes us to lift up ourselves, and to despise others, as if we only were the people in favor with Heaven.[135]

True! What is a leader without followers? How can leaders accomplish by themselves all that God wants accomplished? That is why Paul writes,

> Now about spiritual gifts brothers, I do not want you to be

ignorant...There are different kinds of gifts, but the same Spirit. There are different kinds of service, but one Lord...The body is a unit, though it is made up of many parts, and though all its parts are many, they form one body...The eye cannot say to the hand, "I don't need you!" And the head cannot say to the feet, "I don't need you!" On the contrary, those parts of the body which seem to be weaker are indispensable...there should be no division in the body, but that its parts should have equal concern for each other. (1 Corinthians 12:1, 4, 12, 21, 25, NIV)[136]

There is simply no place for pride or arrogance among God-appointed leaders. As Billy Graham wrote,

The qualifications of a leader are listed several times in the New Testament. He must not be dictatorial, egotistical, or dogmatic; he is to be anything but that. Rather he is to be humble, gracious, courteous, kind, and filled with love; yet at times he must be very firm...Further, the leadership idea outlined in the New Testament is decisively in opposition to the notion of great pomp and pageantry. Rather it emphasizes the graces of humility and service.[137]

Graham's comment, though, makes the point that a leader must be firm. While humility and lack of pride are essential in a leader, a leader must strike the balance between humility and strength. The last thing people want is a weak leader. General Carl von Clausewitz, in his classic work *Principles of War*, considered firmness essential to a military leader; he wrote, "We must never lack the calmness and firmness, which are so hard to preserve in time of war. Without them the most brilliant qualities of mind are wasted."[138] People want leaders of passion and purpose, those who press forward in spite of the obstacles and in spite of hardship. Former Air Force Chief of Staff, General Ronald Fogleman stated, "Good leaders are people with a passion to succeed."[139] Likewise, Spurgeon once stated, "Let each man find out what God wants him to do, and then let him do it, or die in the attempt."[140] This requires a true passion and dedication, a strength and a firmness.

With a God-given leadership comes also a God-given responsibility, and that should put the passion into leaders that followers are looking for. The Blackabys were very right when they wrote,

Spiritual leaders know they must give an account of their

leadership to God; therefore, they are not satisfied merely moving toward the destination God has for them; they want to see God actually achieve his purposes through them for their generation.[141]

This is also what separates spiritually driven leaders from those who are not: They are driven by a sense of the eternal, not by annual or quarterly goals. They should be driven, indeed, but not for themselves or for their own achievements, but for that which God considers important and worth pursuing. "The gift of the Holy Spirit," wrote the Blackabys, "is primarily about God and his work, not about you and your work."[142]

CHAPTER 7
Is Evangelism The Ultimate Goal?

Again, while the thought that a spiritual gift such as leadership may be used in the secular world as well as in the spiritual world, if indeed there is such as separation, there is an apparent quandary for those in leadership roles as to what extent they can use their position of influence for spiritual matters. The question is asked frequently, "Should I use my position as commander for witnessing to those in my unit?"

The quandary comes from a prohibition in the military from commanders, and those in any position of authority, to use that position for proselytizing. An official US Air Force publication states it explicitly:

> Military members must remember that religious choice is a matter of individual conscience. Professionals, and especially commanders, must not take it upon themselves to change or coercively influence the religious views of subordinates.[143]

At face value, then, this is a problem for Christian leaders and a restriction from following the Great Commission which Christ himself gave us. The question seems to be, which do we follow – official military policy or Scriptural mandates? And therefore, is each devout military leader a potential martyr for the faith or does one have to compromise one's faith in order to succeed in the military? Certainly there are implied if not explicit prohibitions in non-military professions as well, so how does one with the spiritual gift of leadership exercise it outside of the church context? Or can one?

Thankfully, this question is entirely moot; it springs from the common ignorance of Scripture and that to which God has called each follower. In fact, leaders in the US military have great freedom to allow the Holy Spirit to manifest himself through them. There need be no compromise, either in one's professionalism as a military member or as a follower of Christ. In fact, the opposite is very true.

So what is it God calls us to, if not to proselytize? The answer is found in two particular passages of Scripture. The first is the Great Commission where Christ says,

> All authority has been to me in heaven and on earth. Go therefore and make disciples of all the nations, baptizing them in the name of the Father and of the Son and of the Holy Spirit, teaching them to observe all things that I have commanded you; and lo, I am with you always, even to the end of the age. (Matthew 28:18-20, NKJV)[144]

There are certain keys to understanding this passage and applying it to military leadership. One is the command, "go." The word "go" does not imply that each one abandon one's vocation in order to become a missionary in a far off country, or even to become a vocational minister. Rick Bereit, author of *In His Service: A Guide to Christian Living In the Military* explains, "The word 'go' ('Go and make disciples') in Matthew 28:18 is more accurately translated, *'having gone on your way'* or *'as you are going on your way.'* This is a present-tense verb implying continuous action."[145] This is yet another indication that the spiritual gift of leadership can and should be used outside of the church context, through any application or vocation, even in the military. As a "continuous action" it implies a lifestyle, not just an occasional act.

But a lifestyle of what? Surprisingly it is not to "witness" in the sense of winning converts who recite the "sinner's prayer" or "give their hearts to Jesus" (terms, by the way, found nowhere in Scripture); it is to make disciples. Discipleship is something which happens along the entire spectrum of faith, whether by influencing a person who has not yet reached a faith in Christ, by being present when a person does reach a faith in Christ, or by influencing a person toward a greater faith in Christ who already has it. Discipleship happens at all stages in a person's life, not just at the point of a saving faith. Paul speaks of these stages when he writes how he and Apollos had different, yet equally as significant roles in the lives of the Corinthians:

> Who then is Paul, and who is Apollos, but ministers through whom you believed, as the Lord gave to each one? I planted, Apollos watered, but God gave the increase. So then neither

he who plants is anything, nor he who waters, but God who gives the increase. Now he who plants and he and waters are one, and each one will receive his own reward according to his labor. (1 Corinthians 3: 5-8, NKJV)[146]

Both Paul and Apollos had work to do along the Corinthians' spectrum of discipleship; neither Paul or Apollos was there, so far as we know, at the time of conversion and yet both did the job of discipleship as assigned, and both would "receive his own reward" for his particular role in it.

Eugene Peterson's paraphrase is even more to the point:

Who do you think Paul is, anyway? Or Apollos for that matter? Servants, both of us – servants who waited on you *as you gradually learned* [emphasis mine] to entrust your lives to our mutual Master. We each carried out our servant assignment. I planted the seed, Apollos watered the plants, but God made you grow. It's not the one who plants or the one who waters who is at the center of the process but God, who makes things grow. Planting and watering are menial servant jobs at minimum wages. What makes them worth doing is the God we are serving. You happen to be in the field *in which we are working* [emphasis mine].[147]

If, then, people are "gradually learning" in the "field in which we are working," whether in a formal ministry, in the military, in politics, in business, in education, or any aspect of life, we are indeed fulfilling the Great Commission, even if we are not present when one in our charge reaches the point of saving faith. As Bereit also wrote, "The ultimate goal was not just to win new believers, but to develop mature disciples."[148]

The second key passage is in the purpose of spiritual gifts as found in Ephesians 4. Here Paul states that each one has received a gift "for the equipping of the saints for the work of ministry, for the edifying of the body of Christ, till we all come to unity of the faith and the knowledge of the Son of God" (Ephesians 4:11-13, NKJV).[149] Leslie Flynn, in his book *19 Gifts of the Spirit*, explains,

The Spirit gave gifts 'for the perfecting of the saints, for the work of ministry, for the edifying of the body of Christ.' This verse seems to indicate that gifts have three purposes, but the punctuation misleads. Both commas interfere with the apostle's meaning. Omit the commas to get the correct sense. Gifts are 'for the perfecting of the saints for the work of the ministry for the edification of the body of Christ.' In other words, gifts prepare saints for the task of ministering in order to build up the body of Christ. Restating it, gifts train servants that they may do the Master's wok, which will then result in the maturing of the church.[150]

> God Opens the Doors
> So far as I know, I have never led someone to Christ as a military leader. Yet I have fulfilled the role of the Great Commission by helping to make disciples. It is amazing how many times a member of my unit has come in, shut the door, and sought spiritual advice! As a commander, I can't preach or proselytize, but if they ask a spiritual question I am free to answer it, and the Lord has provided me opportunities to minister to members of my units within those rules.

Once again, the purpose is to "train" servants, and a synonym for "training" is discipleship. Both a believer's role in the fulfillment of the Great Commission and the believer's goal in the exercise of spiritual gifts is for discipleship. It is not for evangelism in the limited sense of winning converts, but to influence all to greater faith regardless of which point on the spectrum of faith a person may be.

So how can military commanders go about doing this? There are a few ways leaders can disciple others along the spectrum of faith without crossing the line of "coercively influencing the religious beliefs of their subordinates."

One is by setting an example. As Bereit points out, ""Both Jesus and Paul *modeled* the behavior and actions they taught. They *used their own lives* as their primary teaching tool."[151] Not only is this idea acceptable under US Air Force policy, but it is also suggested in the USAF Core Values publication:

> The leader of an organization is key to the moral climate. As does the commander, so does the organization...Leaders cannot just be good; they must be sensitive to their status as role models for their people.[152]

US Air Force Colonel David L. Goldfein reiterated this sentiment when he wrote,

> Integrate the core values into your squadron every day. If you expect your troops to live by these, you must live by them. I once had a commander who made reference to the core values in every corrective action he took – it was very effective.[153]

Likewise, Retired Army Colonel John G. Meyer, Jr. wrote,

> As a commander, you're a role model every minute of every
> day of your command. Soldiers need and want to be led; they
> look to you for guidance. Be a model…The most important
> attribute for success is leading by example. If you lead by
> example in everything you do, you'll succeed. Be a second-to-
> none role model to your officers, NCOs, and soldiers. They'll
> willingly follow a leader who lives both a "do as I say" *and* "do
> as I do" attitude. [154]

Certainly this should go without saying that the leader must model the
behavior he or she seeks in the unit. After all, a leader who fails to model
the standard is merely a hypocrite, whether attempting to disciple people
toward a greater knowledge of Christ or not. All leaders must be modelers.
Christian leaders should model Christ.

Also, as stated before, Christian leaders need to search for opportunities
to bring glory to God. Spurgeon wrote, "Our chief end is to glorify God.
We do not regard it as our first business to convert sinners, nor to edify
the saints; but to glorify God." [155] This is stated by a man who was a very
well-known evangelist of his day, that "converting sinners" is not so much
our mission as to glorify God. Matthew Henry strongly agrees that this
is our main purpose as leaders: "Note, however much we have to do of
business, we must not omit what we have to do for the glory of God, for
that is our best business." [156]

Leaders, too, can disciple those in their charge by following Christ's
command to love each other. Note, as Wayne Grudem wrote, how Christ
influenced all people by loving them:

> Moreover, we have the example of Jesus who did not attempt
> to heal only those who accepted him as Messiah. Rather,
> when great crowds came to him, 'he laid his hands on every
> one of them and healed them' (Luke 4:40). This should give
> us encouragement to carry out deeds of kindness, and to pray
> for healing and other needs, in the lives of unbelievers as well
> as believers. [157]

Leaders in the military will be virtually surrounded by those who are
in dire need of Christ's love, and in this Christian leaders find a golden
opportunity. Leaders can influence their followers greatly by loving them
through "deeds of kindness" and prayer. In fact, even if there ever were a
prohibition in military policy that forbids or discourages open statements

of faith, a Christian leader in the military need not worry, for by showing love to his or her subordinates a leader can communicate his or her faith far more than spoken words can. As Christ himself said, *"By this* [emphasis mine] all will know that you are my disciples, if you have love for one another"* (John 13:35, NKJV).[158] It is not by words or policies, nor even solely by success as a leader, through which leaders communicate that they follow Christ, but through loving those in their charge the way Christ loved his disciples and the crowds around him.

This is not only theoretically possible, but it is a method in practice all over the world where missionaries cannot, by law of the land in which they live, openly proselytize. They instead love those whom they come across in their lives through meeting their personal needs and allow the Holy Spirit to impact them wherever they may be on the spectrum of discipleship. If military commanders view their commands as mission fields this same way, they can find many opportunities to fulfill the Great Commission.

Ultimately, is this not then the ultimate charge of a leader, whether in the ministry or in the military? Our commission from Christ is not so much to win converts but to influence all toward a greater knowledge of himself. Discipleship of all, regardless of where on the spectrum of faith they may be, is the mission of the leader called by the Holy Spirit. As the Blackabys so eloquently wrote,

> The ultimate goal of spiritual leadership is not to achieve numerical results alone, or to do things with perfection, or even to grow for the sake of growth. It is to take their people from where they are to where God wants them to be. God's primary concern for all people is not results but relationship. People's call to be on a right relationship with God takes precedence over their occupation. Calling comes before vocation.[159]

And this, they also write, is perfectly acceptable under military rules which prohibit using one's position to proselytize. If a leader can impact followers through action, modeling, and love, the leader need not pursue the matter any more. The Holy Spirit can at this point step in and take care of the rest. The Blackabys summarize:

> As people grow in their relationship with God, they will hear from God themselves and want to follow him. No one will have to cajole them or entice them into following. It will be a natural heart response. The key to spiritual leadership, then,

is to encourage followers to grow in their relationship with their Lord.[160]

Encouraging followers to grow in their relationship with their Lord, regardless of what that relationship is at the moment, is the complete fulfillment of the Great Commission as well as the fulfillment of the use of the spiritual gift of leadership.

CHAPTER 8
Can One Acquire The Gift Of Leadership?

The common question about leadership is whether leaders are made or born. Certainly a natural talent may come at birth, but a spiritual gift is a different matter. Scripture makes it very clear that leadership, or any spiritual gift, may be acquired over time. Paul commands the Corinthians to "earnestly desire the best gifts" (I Corinthians 12: 31, NKJV)[161] and also to "pursue love and desire spiritual gifts" (1 Corinthians 14: 1, NKJV).[162] Paul later counsels them, "Let him who speaks in a tongue pray that he may interpret" (I Corinthians 14: 13, NKJV),[163] implying that one may acquire spiritual gifts in order to complement others. It seems clear, then, that gifts are not static but can be added to and increased. Matthew Henry wrote, "Gifts are a fit object of our desire and pursuit."[164] Oswald Sanders stated to the same effect. "People without natural leadership skills do not become great leaders at the moment of conversion. Yet a review of the history of the church reveals that the Holy Spirit sometimes releases gifts and qualities that were dormant beforehand."[165]

Indeed, the question may not so much be if a person can acquire additional spiritual gifts such as the gift of leadership, but more when a person will acquire such gifts. Billy Graham wrote, "The process of discovering our spiritual gifts may be a lengthy one, and we may even find gifts emerging as the years go by and we confront new opportunities and challenges."[166] Apparently, as the Holy Spirit leads his followers through different stages, he will also equip them accordingly, and he is by no means bound to lead us through stages according to what gifts we currently have.

Once again, the key is to remember what a spiritual gift is. A gift is an ability given by the Holy Spirit through which he will manifest himself; it has very little to do with what skills we naturally possess. If the Holy Spirit calls a believer to a role or ministry, whether in the church or in the military, Scripture assures us that he will also equip that person accordingly. As Flynn wrote, "A believer would not hold a divinely appointed office without possessing the corresponding gift"[167] and most people would readily agree to that. Yet it is likely that many interpret this as meaning that God will not appoint someone to a leadership position if they don't already have the gift instead of understanding that God will equip the believer with the gift when he appoints the office. The Blackabys make a great point: "Could you imagine the Master giving an order to the servant and the servant replying, 'Sorry, that isn't my gift'?"[168] But surely this happens frequently, even in the Scriptures. When God appointed Moses to lead Israel, Moses' objections to the appointment were no doubt valid. Yet for every objection God provided a solution. The Blackabys made an excellent point when they wrote,

> Arguably the greatest leader in Old Testament history was Moses. However, he could not attribute his success to his own leadership abilities, for he was not naturally gifted as a leader. By his own admission, he was a poor public speaker (Exodus 4:10); he was inept at delegating (Exodus 18: 13-27); he had a temper problem (Exodus 32:19; Numbers 20:9-13). Worst of all, he was a murderer. Nevertheless, Moses' accomplishments as a spiritual leader came from the depth of his relationship with God, not from the strength of his personality.[169]

We can see here, as Henry pointed out, God often times specifically chooses those who don't already have natural ability, or those in whom the ability to lead is latent and unnoticed, to be the leaders he desires. As he stated of Moses' commission:

> The difficulties of the work were indeed very great, enough to startle the courage and stagger the faith of Moses himself. Note, even wise and faithful instruments may be much discouraged at the difficulties that lie in the way...Yet Moses is the man that does it at last, for God gives grace to the lowly. Modest beginnings are very good presages. God answers the objection. He promises his presence: *Certainly I will be with thee*, and that is enough. Note, those that are weak in themselves may yet do wonders, being strong in the Lord and in the power of his might; and those that are most diffident of themselves

may be most confident in God. God's presence puts an honour upon the worthless, wisdom and strength to the weak and foolish, makes the greatest difficulties dwindle to nothing, and is enough to answer all objections.[170]

The Blackabys have seen this in recent times and wrote,

> We hear people complaining about the talents and skills they lack, then concluding, 'I don't have anything to offer God.' That's likely true, but what does that have to do with the Holy Spirit working in your life? When He's present, it doesn't matter what *you* can do or cannot do. If you don't have a lot of natural talent, you can know that before God you're the perfect vessel for Him to show Himself in you. Listen to his promise: 'My grace is sufficient for you, for My strength is made perfect in weakness' (2 Corinthians 12:9). In your weakness, He is strong. *You* are the person in whom He can do His best work, for He will get all the glory.[171]

So indeed, the Holy Spirit may very well call someone to a position of leadership who is by no means naturally equipped for it. Additionally, the Holy Spirit may call someone to a greater leadership role who is not in himself equal to that challenge. Yet we need not fear; when God calls, he will also equip. As the Blackabys commented:

> As the Spirit reveals the will of the Father, we can then allow Him to accomplish it through our lives by the Spirit's enabling. *Equipping always follows the assignment.* The enabling power of the Holy Spirit folows the assignment, never precedes it.[172]

John Borek, Danny Lovett and Elmer Towns concur. They wrote, "Effective leaders understand 'the gifts and the calling of God are irrevocable' (Romans. 11:29). God's call on the life of a leader is His guarantee of assistance. 'He who calls you is faithful, who also will do it' (1 Thessalonians. 5:24)."[173] Oswald Sanders agreed and stated that, while a person may be taking on a challenge greater than himself, this should give the believer great confidence. He wrote, "The sovereign selection of God gives great confidence to Christian workers. We can truly say, 'I am here neither by selection of an individual nor election of a group, but by the almighty appointment of God."[174]

It is good to know that spiritual gifts, to include leadership, are not static. They will grow and mature as God calls leaders to greater leadership challenges. If the expectation of leaders in the US Army is, "Your leadership skills will improve as your experience broadens,"[175] then the comfort of the Scriptures, according to Rick Warren is, "Whatever gifts you have been given can be enlarged and developed through practice."[176]

This should be a great source of encouragement to military members since every person, regardless of natural leadership ability, is expected to become a leader. Former Commandant of the US Marine Corps, General CB Coates, once stated, "Inherent [leadership] ability obviously cannot be instilled but that which is latent or dormant can be developed. The average good man in our Service is and must be considered a potential leader."[177] This expectation grows as each member is expected to demonstrate greater

---

God in Baghdad

When I served in Baghdad, even though I was in the Air Force, I had to lead ground action in the International Zone (often referred to as the "Green Zone"). One time, when I was directed to lead a raid of a house in an Iraqi neighborhood to capture some insurgents, I put it to the Lord to guide my leadership. Our plan was good and our execution was flawless, and we succeeded in capturing the people we were after. However, in the middle of the raid, an Iraqi man talking on a cell phone wandered into our operation. I wanted to be careful not to involve any innocent people, and I got frustrated when he kept walking into our area. When my apprehension team pounced on him, handcuffed him and hauled him off to the rear, some of my intel gatherers, who had been observing the neighborhood all afternoon prior to the raid told me to make sure we turned this man in, since he had been in the house earlier in the day. As it turns out, this man was our biggest catch, and had been wanted by our intelligence officers – we caught him by accident! As I congratulated my apprehension team on bagging such a huge find they complemented me on having the insight to give the order to capture him. I would have had reason to be proud of myself, too, except that I never gave that order. As clearly as they heard me give it, I know I never did. As I reflected on it, the Holy Spirit let me know he was the one behind my success. My plan was good, but the success he gave me made it better, and in a way I knew I could not take credit for it. Maybe only He and I knew the truth, but I saw the Holy Spirit in action that day in Baghdad.

---

and greater leadership as he or she advances through the ranks and through various assignments. Yet, as God calls his people in the military to those different assignments, it is He who will give the ability necessary to meet the new and greater demands. The challenge for those in the military is, as they are searching for that next assignment, to not be dissuaded by the increased leadership demands if they feel the prompting of the Holy Spirit. The Blackabys ask a great question which is applicable to this stage in the life of military leaders. "Do you make your decisions based upon your ability to achieve the results," they ask, "or upon the Spirit's leading and equipping?"[178] Indeed, the latter should be the rule: "The Holy Spirit empowers believers in the Christian life and service," wrote Erikson. "Personal inadequacies should not deter us or discourage us."[179]

In fact, the opposite is true: We should not only not avoid leadership challenges beyond our ability, we should expect them. The Blackabys pointed out, "If we operate only according to our talents and ability, we get the glory."[180] If this is true, then in order for the Holy Spirit to manifest himself and reveal himself through us, then he must take us to and through demands of leadership greater than that to which we are equal.

A poignant example of military leadership in Scripture which demonstrates how God's equipping comes with His call is Gideon. Like Moses, Gideon had plenty of good reason not be called as a leader. The Blackabys wrote of Gideon,

> When the Lord gave him an assignment, Gideon's response was honest: 'O my Lord, how can I save Israel? Indeed my clan is the weakest in Manasseh, and I am the least in my father's house' (Judges 6:15). Gideon was right; he had no abilities that would enable him to lead the people into battle.[181]

It is clear, actually, that Gideon was really the antithesis of a potentially great military leader. He was of the smallest of the tribes, and as the youngest of his family he probably would not have been singled out for any specialized military or leadership training. The Blackabys humorously comment, "If Gideon had taken a spiritual gift inventory to determine his future course of action, his chances for taking a job as a military general would be almost nil."[182] Yet God's rationale for choosing Gideon wasn't simply to win the battle but to manifest himself; if this was the case then a person not naturally endowed with leadership ability was God's best alternative. "'But the Spirit of the LORD came upon Gideon' (Judges 6:34), and God's power was displayed through him and his men."[183]

It is clear, then, that one can acquire the gift of leadership if he or she doesn't have it in the same way that those who have the gift of leadership can expect their abilities to be constantly tried and strengthened through challenges. To acquire the gift or to have it enhanced is the desire and the work of God.

The spiritual gift of leadership is highly misunderstood and therefore it is probably also not applied fully, whether by those in ministry who don't know they have it or by those not in ministry who don't know they can have it. Yet an understanding of what it is shows us how it is purely the Holy Spirit manifesting himself through the leadership skills a person has, and this can apply to ministry, the military, or any leadership role into which the Holy Spirit will call his people. To understand its purpose shows that a person can and should exercise the gift without any fear of spiritual or professional compromise. To understand how one acquires it and strengthens it shows that the Holy Spirit will equip his leaders equal to the challenge through which he has called them to lead in order to show himself to the world.

PART III
The Cost of Leadership: Sacrifice is Not an Option

In Luke 14, Jesus spoke words which every aspiring leader should consider prior to pursuing a leadership role.

> Which of you, intending to build a tower, does not sit down first and count the cost, whether he has enough to finish it, lest after he has laid the foundation, and is not able to finish, all who see it begin to mock him, saying, "This man began to build and was not able to finish." (Luke 14:28-30, NKJV)[184]

While this verse may seem like a simple lesson out of any basic management class which tells an aspiring manager not to go into debt or to ensure one has the resources to do the job, the application is actually far more profound when applied to leadership. In this passage, Jesus isn't doing a discourse on real estate development; looking at it in its context we can see how he is really asking his followers which ones were really willing to pay the price for the distinction of being his disciple. In the same way, aspiring leaders, even those potentially called by the Lord to leadership, need to do just as our Lord suggests – each needs to weigh the costs of leadership and decide if he or she really wants to pay the price.

Many aspire to the position of leadership. They are drawn by the honor, the respect, and the satisfaction of getting a job done. For some, it is a quest for power. Many are drawn to military leadership by the vision of gloriously leading a charge in battle, earning medals, or attaining high rank. Yet those who seek to lead for any of these reasons clearly do not understand the nature of leadership. Oswald Sanders wrote clearly, "To aspire to leadership...requires us to be willing to pay a price higher than others are willing to pay. The toll of leadership is heavy, and the more effective the leadership, the higher it goes."[185]

Leadership, at its core, is sacrifice. Leaders do not lead to gain; the nature of leadership is to give. John Maxwell wrote, "Many people today want to climb up the corporate ladder because they believe that freedom and power are the prizes waiting at the top. They don't realize that the true nature of leadership is sacrifice."[186] Maxwell also stated, "Ninety-five percent of achieving anything is knowing what you want and paying the price to get it."[187] For the leader, the price to be paid is sacrificing oneself, sacrificing personal prestige, and sacrificing one's ambition. Unless a person is willing to pay this price, he or she should not aspire to leadership.

CHAPTER 9
Sacrifice Of Self

Successful leadership comes at a personal cost. A leader must be willing to give of himself for the good of the organization and for the good of those in his organization. This is not just a one-time or even frequent sacrifice – it is a constant sacrifice. "This part of leadership," Oswald Sanders wrote of self-sacrifice, "must be paid daily."[188]

A leader must be willing to sacrifice popularity and being well-liked. In fact, leadership by its very definition is loneliness. Charles Stanley, referring to the gift of leadership spoken of in 1 Corinthians 12, wrote, "The Greek word [for leading, ruling, or the gift of administration] literally means 'the one who stands out front.'"[189] Note that he uses the definite article, "*the* one who stands out front." Leadership is not a group function. There is one leader and that one person stands out in front alone.

One must never confuse popularity with being an effective leader. As Peter Drucker stated, "Popularity is not leadership. Results are."[190] Certainly, one can be popular and effective as a leader, but they are far from synonymous. Moses was an exceptionally effective leader, but there were periods when he was far from being the people's choice of a leader. In fact, at one point he cried out to God, "What shall I do with this people? They are almost ready to stone me!" (Exodus 17: 4, NKJV).[191] Likewise, Gideon was faithful to God's call to remove the altars of Baal and in doing so became so exceedingly unpopular that Gideon's neighbors demanded of his father, "Bring out your son, that he may die, because he has torn down the altar of Baal, and because he has cut down the wooden image that was beside it" (Judges 6: 30, NKJV).[192] David had his life threatened many times, by both his enemies whom he threatened in battle, and by some of his own countrymen who were jealous of his position. Even family members opposed him throughout his life. As Colonel (US Army, Retired) John G. Meyer, Jr. wrote to aspiring junior officers in his book *Company Command: The Bottom Line*, "Command can be lonely. But remember, you weren't selected to be a company commander to win a popularity contest."[193]

This does not imply that a leader must isolate himself to be effective or that cruelty toward one's followers is acceptable, but effective leadership does not allow the luxury of blending into the crowd. Indeed, the leader must determine to be "the one" who stands out in front of the followers. Sanders made it clear,

> Because the leader must always be ahead of his followers, he lives with loneliness. Though he may be friendly, there are areas of life where he must walk alone...The leader must be a person who, while welcoming the friendship and support of all who offer it, has sufficient inner resources to stand alone – even in the face of stiff opposition to have "no one but God."[194]

As "the one" who is to be in front, the leader must be willing to bear the complete responsibility for the success or failure of the mission. The leader must be willing to make the decisions and bear the consequences. If the leader cannot say, "The buck stops here," then he or she is not suited for the job.

Ironically, while leadership results in loneliness, it also means the loss of privacy. If one looks at the qualifications of the leaders of the early church as directed by the Apostle Paul to Timothy, one can see that every aspect of the leaders' lives are open for all to see and critique:

> A bishop must be blameless, the husband of one wife, temperate, sober-minded, of good behavior, hospitable, able to teach; not given to wine, not violent, not greedy for money, but gentle, not quarrelsome, not covetous; one who rules his own house well, having his children in submission with all reverence (for if a man does not know how to rule his own house, how will he take care of the church of God?)...Moreover, he must have a good testimony among those who are outside, lest he fall into reproach and the snare of the devil (I Timothy 3:1-7, NKJV).[195]

Clearly, a leader's whole life is under scrutiny from the beginning and throughout his time as a leader. Everything from personality to motives to family life to behavior is essentially an open book. Colonel Meyer asked a tough question of those looking to take on company command, "Are you willing to lead by example in everything you do – to live in a fish bowl with your personal and professional life open to view?"[196] This is a good question for all leaders because leadership demands it. There is no separating professional from personal as a leader.

At the same time, a leader must sacrifice many of life's pleasures and personal time for the sake of his followers and the success of the organization. A leader must be ahead and remain ahead in thought, knowledge, and ability in order to be effective, and these demand more and more of one's private time. General S.L.A. Marshall once commented,

> Personal advancement within any worthwhile system requires some sacrifice of leisure and more careful attention to the better organization of one's working routine. But that does not demand self-sacrifice or the forfeiting of any of life's truly enduring rewards. It means putting the convenient excuse for postponing solution of the problem until the next time. It means cultivating the mind during hours that would otherwise be spent at idleness. It means concentrating for longer periods on the work at hand without getting up from one's chair... Here is the great part of the secret. It is in the exercise of the will that the men are separated from the boys, from the one who is truly ambitions to become superior in his life calling.[197]

Truly, a leader must be willing to allow every aspect of his life to be open to scrutiny and to give up his private time to mature as a leader and for the good of those in his charge.

Additionally, a leader must be willing to suffer. This idea is dramatically different from the visualized concept of a leader, especially in the military – the one who is praised, lionized, and constantly rewarded for success and service. Much to the contrary, leadership involves suffering to some extent.

On one end of the spectrum, the leader is always the first to receive criticism from detractors. In more intense or violent confrontations, resistance will always target the leader. Sanders pointed out that historically, "The leader was the first to draw fire in persecution, the first in line to suffer"[198] and this brings a whole new meaning to the idea of being "the one who stands out in front." James Kouzes and Barry Posner agree. "Leaders who are truly inspirational, who demonstrate courage and passion" they wrote, "are the first to suffer."[199] In a more light-hearted way of putting it, B.R. Lakin stated, "If you want to avoid criticism, just be

Paul D. Cairney

nothing, say nothing, and do nothing. As long as they are kicking you in the behind, you know you are still out front."[200]

Sacrifice is gain

It took me years to understand Jesus' parables of the treasure in the field and the pearl of great price (Matthew 13). Both are about sacrifice. One man sold everything he had to buy a field which contained a great treasure, and the other sold everything he had to buy a valuable pearl. I didn't understand this until I realized that both men knew that, although they were giving up everything, they were in turn gaining so much more. This is the nature of sacrifice – not giving something up just for the sake of doing it and being miserable about it, but giving up something knowing that the cost is little compared to the gain. This is how leaders can sacrifice of themselves joyfully and not as martyrs, when they know that the results of their sacrifices can be far more than what they give up.

If leaders do not suffer from resistance and persecution, leaders will suffer physically because of pure weariness. Again, while the image of a leader is that of a king surrounded and doted upon by servants or a general surrounded by staff officers who run to do his bidding, these are far from the reality of leadership. Sanders stated, "Fatigue is the cost of leadership. Mediocrity is the result of never getting tired."[201] A leader should expect to face exhaustion. Note too Paul's comment to Timothy that "If a man desires the position of bishop, he desires a good work" (1 Timothy 3:1, NKJV)[202]; he doesn't say that the person desires a good position or job title—that much is obvious—but that he desires a good work. Hard, tiring, and frustrating work is the lot of a leader. It is work that not all are suited to do. It is work that is necessary for the success of the organization. Richard and Henry Blackaby stated rightly, "The bottom line is this: Leadership is hard work. There are no short-cuts. Some people look for easy paths to leadership positions. They want positions of influence, but they don't want to put in their time in the trenches."[203] Simply, those who do not wish to do work should no aspire to the position of a leader.

As another aspect of suffering, Sanders wrote, "Scars are the authenticating marks of faithful leadership and true spiritual leadership"[204] and he was probably more right than even he knew, since in some cases the scars are literal physical and not just figurative or psychological scars. W. Brad Johnson and Gary Harper wrote that in the military sense,

64

physical scars always came first to the leaders, and for none was this more true than for the senior officers of the prisoners of war held in captivity in North Viet Nam. They pointed out, "The rules in the 'Hanoi Hilton' were quite simple. 'To lead was to be tortured. To communicate with a fellow prisoner was a *de facto* sign of leadership that resulted in torture."[205] How many aspiring leaders are willing to accept this price of leadership? Are they willing to forego the brass, braid, and decorations in exchange for bruises?

Many people erroneously picture leaders as those who are the most gifted and who are therefore immune to struggle. Yet again this is far from true. Regardless of the extent of a leader's natural attributes and skills, the leader will experience hardship and suffering. As Sanders wrote,

> Many people regard leaders as naturally gifted with intellect, personal forcefulness, and enthusiasm. Such qualities certainly enhance leadership potential, but they do not define the spiritual leader. True leaders must be willing to suffer for the sake of the objectives great enough to demand their wholehearted obedience.[206]

Leaders must be willing to sacrifice their very selves in order to be effective. This is a condition, not an option, of leadership.

CHAPTER 10
Sacrifice Of Prestige:
Servant Leadership

If there is another image of leadership which is the antithesis of that to which Scripture calls people, it is that of the dictatorial and forceful leader, or the one who exalts himself over his followers. In fact, Scripture calls leaders to the exact opposite. Henry and Richard Blackaby state as a warning to potential leaders,

> Some Christian leaders believe that God delegates his authority to leaders and that followers are obligated to submit to them unquestioningly as if they were obeying God…Christian leaders also invite rebellion when they use force to achieve their organizational goals.[207]

Christ spoke of the same misunderstanding of leadership which he observed and ultimately confronted during his time on Earth. Though telling his disciples that they were still obligated to follow the leadership of the religious establishment of the day, he warned them against emulating their style.

> Then Jesus spoke to the multitudes and to His disciples, saying: The scribes and Pharisees sit in Moses' seat. Therefore whatever they tell you to observe, that observe and do, but do not do according to their works; for they say, and do not do. For they bind heavy burdens, hard to bear, and lay them on men's shoulders; but they themselves will not move them with one of their fingers. But all their works they do to be seen by men. They make their phylacteries broad and enlarge the borders

of their garments. They love the best places at feasts, the best seats in the synagogue, greetings in the marketplaces…But he who is greatest among you shall be your servant. (Matthew 23: 1-7,11, NKJV)[208]

It is clear that Christ prescribed an attitude of service for his leaders. They were to be willing to sacrifice the image and prestige of the position in order to be the most effective leaders they could be. The prescription is as clear today as it was then. As Eugene Peterson paraphrases Christ's words in *The Message*, "Do you want to stand out? Then step down. Be a servant" (Matthew 23:11, *The Message*).[209]

Christ's closest disciples were lured by the over-glorified concept of being leaders in Christ's kingdom and had to rethink what they had to look forward to.

Then James and John, the sons of Zebedee, came to him. "Teacher," they said, "we want you to do for us whatever we ask." "What do you want me to do for you?" he asked. They replied, "Let one of us sit at your right and the other at your left in your glory." "You don't know what you are asking," Jesus said. "Can you drink the cup I drink or be baptized with the baptism I am baptized with?" "We can," they answered. Jesus said to them, "You will drink the cup I drink and be baptized with the baptism I am baptized with, but to sit at my right or left is not for me to grant. These places belong to those for whom they have been prepared." When the ten heard about this, they became indignant with James and John. Jesus called them together and said, "You know that those who are regarded as rulers of the Gentiles lord it over them, and their high officials exercise authority over them. Not so with you. Instead, whoever wants to become great among you must be your servant, and whoever wants to be first must be slave of all. For even the Son of Man did not come to be served, but to serve, and to give his life as a ransom for many (Mark 10:35-45, NIV).[210]

As Sanders observed of this passage, "James and John wanted the glory, but not the cup of shame; the crown, but not the cross; the role of master, but not the servant."[211] They wanted to share in the glory Christ would ultimately have as King, but they did not yet understand that a leader must accept the "cup of shame" before he could expect any reward for his leadership. This is also a message a leader will find throughout the Scriptures, not just in this passage. Sanders pointed out that, "The King James Bible uses the term *leader* only six times. Much more frequently, the role is called *servant*. We do not read about 'Moses, my leader,' but 'Moses, my servant.' And this is exactly what Christ taught."[212]

Spurgeon suggested the same sort of title change for leaders in the church in order to emphasize the point that a leader is called to be a servant first before he could expect any sort of reward. As he stated,

> We are ministers. The word has a very respectable sound. To be a minister is the aspiration of many a youth. Perhaps if the word were otherwise rendered, their ambition might cool. Ministers are servants; they are not guests, but waiters; not landlords, but labourers.[213]

This creates quite a paradigm shift. Leaders are accustomed to deference and good treatment as natural trappings of the office, but this is not what Christ calls us to in this passage, nor is it what the entire Scripture speaks of for those called by God to leadership.

Indeed this is a radical paradigm shift. Leadership studies today call for a leader to be confident and have a "take charge personality," and while these are true Scripture also states that humility is a prerequisite for effective leadership. Pride and arrogance have no place in the leadership style of one called by the Holy Spirit to lead. Leaders need to recognize that they are called to leadership not because of their own merits or worth but simply by the sovereign decision of the Holy Spirit. David Howard stated on this fact, "God has not called a spiritual elite to carry out the work of ministry, bypassing the ordinary believer in the church. Rather 'to each is given the manifestation of the Spirit for the common good.' (I Corinthians 12:7)"[214] The leader called by the Holy Spirit must shun pride and a sense of self-sufficiency, realizing that his followers are likewise called by the Holy Spirit to fulfill their own functions. When a leader forgets the empowerment comes from the Holy Spirit, not only to himself but to those he leads, the results can lead to ruin. As the Blackabys stated,

> Pride causes Christian leaders to take the credit not only for what their people have done but also for what God has accomplished. Spiritual leaders are God's servants, but pride can cause them to act as if God were their servant, obligated to answer their selfish prayers and to bless their grandiose schemes.[215]

This is precisely why sometimes the most effective leader is the one who is not naturally talented or perhaps has no personal desire to lead. The one who is not naturally talented as a leader will more likely remain reliant on the Holy Spirit for strength, for guidance, and for results. Likewise, the one who must be drawn into leadership by the Holy Spirit is also the most humble because he is not seduced by the prestige or power but leads purely out of obedience to Christ. As A.W. Tozer stated,

> A true and safe leader is likely to be one who has no desire to lead, but is forced into a position by the inward pressure of the Holy Spirit and the press of [circumstances]...There was hardly a great leader from Paul to the present day but was drafted by the Holy Spirit for the task, and commissioned by the Lord to fill a position he had little heart for...The man who is ambitious to lead is disqualified as a leader. The true leader will have no desire to lord it over God's heritage, but will be humble, gentle, self-sacrificing and altogether ready to follow when the Spirit chooses another to lead."[216]

Again, this seems the opposite of the picture of a strong leader, especially in the military setting where brass, braids, decorations and protocol seem to mark the most effective leaders. Yet even in the military, humility marks an effective and respected leader. Historian James McPherson spoke of a prevailing attitude in the Civil War which can be just as applicable today, that when it comes to the quality of a person a follower is just as good as a leader; this leaves the leader little room to "lord it over" his followers. He wrote,

> The affection of enlisted men for officers who would lend them a horse or carry a gun suggests an important truth: in these democratic citizen armies "the men think themselves as good as their officer," wrote a lieutenant recently promoted from the ranks in the 1st Connecticut Cavalry, "and I suppose they are." When officers flaunted their rank and acted like they were better than privates, the latter resented it and made their dislike of such officers abundantly clear.[217]

Indeed, the military officer who "flaunts his rank" and affects superiority over his followers is only deceiving himself as to his effectiveness. Ironically, he is probably damaging his effectiveness by using this approach. As Rick Bereit wrote as advice for military officers,

Jesus told his disciples that the power-wielding, abusive leadership they were used to was not part of God's plan. In His plan for godly leadership, those who served would become the great ones…As we carefully consider his command and His example, it's easy to see the merit in the method. A leader who extracts performance by force and positional power achieves, at best, exactly what he asks for and no more. A leader who guides with wisdom, while looking out for the needs of his people, will be surprised at the levels of performance subordinates achieve. A selfless leader earns trust from his followers.[218]

Every leader wants to achieve the maximum amount possible, and clearly the way not to accomplish this is by being overbearing and arrogant. As much as current thinking lauds a dictatorial and self-promoting approach, both Scripture and reason tell us otherwise. As Sanders wrote,

Christ told his disciples to turn away from the pompous attitudes of the oriental despots, and instead take on the lowly bearing of the servant. As in ancient days, so today humility is the least admired in political and business circles. But no bother! The spiritual leader will choose the hidden path of sacrificial service and approval of the Lord over flamboyant self-advertising in the world.[219]

But what really is humility? Is it a sense or mentality that one is insufficient and worthless with nothing to contribute? Probably not. In fact, there may be some wisdom to Sherlock Holmes' reply when his chronicler Dr. Watson spoke of modesty as a virtue.

"My dear Watson," said he, "I cannot agree with those who rank modesty among the virtues. To the logician all things should be seen exactly as they are, and to underestimate oneself is as much a departure from the truth as to exaggerate one's own powers."[220]

Holmes was probably right. One needs to know and acknowledge if one has a gift such as leadership and to what extent one has it if one is to be able to effectively employ it. Matthew Henry would have agreed with Sherlock Holmes; he wrote,

As we must not on one hand be proud of our talents, so on the other hand we must not bury them. We must not say, "I am nothing, therefore I will sit still and do nothing'; but, 'I am

71

nothing in myself, and therefore I will extend myself to the utmost in the strength of the grace of Christ."[221]

To understand what humility is, we can start by understanding what humility is not. Humility is not a synonym for insecurity or sense of worthlessness. As the Blackabys wrote, "Insecurity and a need for affirmation drive some people to seek leadership positions. A telling sign of such leaders is their intolerance toward anyone who challenges them."[222] They are very right in this; an insecure person in a position of authority will probably overcompensate for his perceived lack of strength by bullying and overpowering his followers, not by listening, allowing constructive criticism, and seeking to understand those who disagree.

Nor on the other hand does humility mean that a leader should allow others to dominate him even if others appear more talented, intelligent, or otherwise. As Paul wrote to Timothy,

> Command and teach these things. Don't let anyone look down on you because you are young, but set an example for the believers I speech, in life, in love, in faith and in purity… Do not rebuke an older man harshly, but exhort him as if he were your father. Treat younger men as brothers, older women as mothers, and younger women as sisters, with absolute purity (I Timothy 4:12, NIV).[223]

Paul did not tell Timothy to submit to those who apparently had greater qualifications than Timothy did, but neither did Paul say to attempt to dominate those people. Timothy was to treat all with respect while still leading them. All leaders may be in charge over people who are more qualified to lead, and yet only the appointed leader has the responsibility of accomplishing the mission. As Colonel Meyers so succinctly stated, "Who's in charge? You are, and don't ever forget it!"[224]

Matthew Henry went back to Romans 12 to come up with a good description of humility. He wrote, quoting Romans 12: 3:

> "For I say, through the grace given to me, to everyone who is among you, not to think of himself more highly than he ought to think, but to think soberly, as God has dealt to each one a measure of faith." We must take heed of having too great an opinion of ourselves. We must not be self-conceited, nor esteem too much our own wisdom. There is a high thought of ourselves too good to be the slaves of sin and drudges to this world. We should think soberly, that is, we must have a modest

option of ourselves and our own abilities, according to what we have received from God, and not otherwise.[225]

Humility is not having "too great an opinion" of oneself and the ability to keep our abilities as leaders in perspective. There is a way to do this, suggested Phillip Brooks in 1872: "The true way to be humble is not to stoop until you are smaller than yourself, but to stand at your real height against some higher nature that will show you what the real smallness of your greatness is."[226] There will always be those with greater and more effective leadership abilities than ourselves, and reflecting what great things God has done through others will help us keep our own egos in check.

It is essential as too, as Henry pointed out, to realize that the leadership ability one has is purely what one has received of God; these are not self-created abilities. Whether a leader is born with them or not is really not the issue; they are given of God. James had to remind his readers as well of that point: *"Every* good gift and *every* perfect gift is from above, and comes down from the Father of lights" [emphasis mine] (James 1: 17, NKJV).[227]

Henry also made an excellent point that leaders are not immune from temptation and sin, and should pride get in the way leaders are probably even more susceptible to the thought that they are immune. Leaders, especially those in the military, are called to discipline those in their charge and in this light Paul wrote to the leaders of the Galatians, "Brethren, if a man is overtaken in a trespass, you who are spiritual restore such a one in a spirit of gentleness, considering yourself lest you also be tempted" (Galatians 6:1, NKJV).[228] Eugene Peterson paraphrased it with great effectiveness: "If someone falls into sin, forgivingly restore him, saving the critical comments for yourself. You might be needing forgiveness before the day's out…If you think you are too good for that, you are badly deceived" (Galatians 6:1, *The Message*).[229] Paul himself apparently struggled with keeping his extraordinary abilities in perspective. "To keep me from becoming conceited," he shared with the Corinthians, "there was given me a thorn in my flesh, a minister of Satan to torment me" (2 Corinthians 12: 7, NIV).[230] Paul was cryptic about what this "thorn" actually was, but Henry suggested that it may have been a temptation to which Paul was particularly susceptible. As Henry wrote,

> We are much in the dark about what this was, whether some great trouble or some great temptation…Temptations to sin are the most grievous thorns, they are messengers of Satan, to

buffet us. Indeed it is a great grievance to a good man to be so much tempted to sin. The design of this was to keep the apostle humble.[231]

This is where Christians need to get rid of any arrogance that thinks that to face temptation is the sign of weakness or spiritual immaturity. In fact, the opposite is true. Rick Warren stated, "Temptation is a sign that Satan hates you, not a sign of weakness or worldliness."[232] Satan will hate a leader more as the leader accomplishes more for God, so it is logical that the more effective a leader the more that leader will face temptation. After all, if a leader is ineffective anyway, why would Satan waste his time?

It is probable, then, that temptation is a tool used by Satan to derail those who are effective for God while at the same time being an opportunity God uses to keep his appointed leaders humble. Leaders will face temptation like no others, and for this reason leaders must be ever so thankful for God's endless grace and forgiveness. "My grace is sufficient for you," our Lord to Paul, "for my power is made perfect in weakness" (2 Corinthians 12: 8, NIV).[233] Leaders will fail, and yet God's grace is enough to overcome those failures, even sin. Leaders should let humility be the result.

Putting others ahead of oneself is also the hallmark of humility. John Maxwell says of humble leaders, "They're not out to prove anything, and they don't care who gets the credit. They're glad to share the spotlight with others when they succeed."[234] They are willing to push others forward into glory and recognition while they themselves remain unnoticed and anonymous.

Humility also involves knowing for whose credit a leader works. Many leaders are ambitious people, and yet to search for one's own glory should not be the goal of leaders. As Charles Haddon Spurgeon wrote,

> The proper recognition of the EGO is a theme worthy of our attention. I will make a word if I may: Let EGOTISM stand for proud, vainglorious, intrusive selfhood, and let EGOISM stand for the humble, responsible, and honest selfhood which, finding itself in being, resolves to be at the Divine bidding, and to be at its best, to the glory of God.[235]

Again, humility is not a failure to acknowledge or a suppression of one's abilities, but a rejection of the "vainglorious, intrusive selfhood" and an embracing of the "honest selfhood" which seeks the glory of God instead of own glory.

Humility, then, is honesty through the proper perspective of one's

---

Cold Feet

While stationed in the United Kingdom, I was responsible for the security of three small Air Force bases and an organization of about 60 enlisted men and women. Toward the end of one fiscal year, we had not spent out our entire annual budget and I was wondering how to best do it. This was nothing out of the ordinary, and this is when many commanders buy up new office furniture and other niceties which they would not ordinarily have budget for as a means of spending their unit's final dollars. I pondered how to spend down my last remaining money as I went out to do "post checks" on my Airmen who were doing entry control at the main gate on a typically cold and rainy British fall day. As I spoke with one of my Airmen inside his gate shack, I realized he was very uncomfortable. "My feet are freezing," he told me. "Once they get wet, they are cold for the rest of the shift." In this case, he had been working outside at his post since around six o'clock that morning wearing his now-saturated issue combat boots. The next day, I told my resource advisor I knew how I wanted to spend down my last remaining funds, and as he pulled out the office furniture catalogues I told him I wanted to buy wet-weather boots for all of the Airmen not working a staff job. He was right when he pointed out that our furniture was old and shoddy and needed replacing, but my mind was made up and so we ordered the boots. It wasn't until a few months later that I saw this same Airman at his post, in the same cold rain, but this time with a big grin on his face as he saw me approach his post. "How are your feet?" I asked. "Dry and warm," he said. I knew I had scored some points, but what I also learned was that as they no longer had to worry about their feet getting wet and cold, they were not spending all of their time inside the gate shack but being outside and vigilant; in other words, they did their jobs even better. I took care of them as people and they accomplished the mission better. What leader could want anything more?

---

abilities and one's limitations, realizing that all are the gift of God. Humility is putting others ahead of ourselves. Humility is working for the glory of God and not for our own benefit. As Larry Michael wrote,

Humility demonstrates a servant's heart. It shows willingness to listen, to learn, to admit when one is wrong... Humility means that one always remains teachable. It means one is willing to let others get the credit...

The secure leader is confidet in his ability to lead and to serve others in the process.[236]

With humility as a foundation, servant leaders also must ensure they put the mission of their organization ahead of their own needs and wants. "The concept of servant leadership, "wrote Larry Michael, "implies that we are more conscious of our responsibilities than our rights."[237] Likewise, as Gerald Brooks stated, "When you become a leader, you lose the right to think about yourself."[238]

In a military setting, this is as true as anywhere. Colonel Meyer wrote that officers who put themselves first are ineffective in command. "For self-servers, command will not be a pleasant experience. They'll do their time, punch their ticket, make no impact, and then move on."[239]

Even worse, as Abraham Zaleznik rightly stated, a self-centered leader will actually be destructive to a military unit.

> A dangerous trend toward careerism has developed…Nothing destroys mutual confidence between a person in authority and the subordinates more than an awareness that the supervisor, executive, or officer is fundamentally looking out for his own self-interest.[240]

But it need not be this way. When a commander focuses on the mission and not on himself, he may find that he has even more motivation. As Kouzes and Posner wrote, "Leaders are those who are serving a purpose and are willing to act on what they believe."[241] Focusing on the mission actually strengthens a leader, they also stated. "In serving a purpose, leaders strengthen credibility by demonstrating that they are not in it for themselves; instead, they have the interests of the institution, department, or team and its constituents at heart."[242]

Second only to focusing on getting the mission done, a leader's focus must be on the people he leads. Oswald Sanders wrote that this is essential for every leader to understand fully.

> At the outset of any study of spiritual leadership, this master principle must be squarely faced: True greatness, true leadership, is found in giving yourself in service to others, not in coaxing or inducing others to serve you. True service is never without cost. Often it comes with a painful baptism of suffering. But the true spiritual leader is focused on the service he and she can render to God and other people, not on the residual perks of high office or holy title.[243]

Kouzes and Posner state this as well. A leader cannot be in it for himself, but must focus on his people.

> In democratic societies, people do not talk about themselves as being subordinate to their leaders. Why should it be any different in our offices and factories? In democratic societies, leaders serve the people's needs and interests. Leaders serve their constituencies.[244]

But what about in a military setting? Can a leader succeed in the military by putting his junior officers, noncommissioned officers and junior enlisted members ahead of himself? Rick Bereit says this is not only possible but it is also required.

> Is it possible to adopt and live out Jesus' value system in today's military? Does the same standard apply to senior NCOs and officers as well as junior officers and lower-ranking enlisted men and women? Yes! It is not only possible, it is required of all who follow Jesus.[245]

How does a leader do this? How does a leader put their subordinates first? One way is by meeting their needs. This, says Bercit, defines a servant. "A servant is one who sees a need and meets it," he wrote, "without being asked and without expecting reward."[246] While it is natural to think of those in the lowest ranks as being the servants, he wrote,

> What about officers and NCOs? Are they expected to serve, too? Yes, and their ability to serve increases with additional authority. A leader serves subordinates by (nothing new here!) seeing the needs and meeting them, without being asked and without expecting reward.[247]

Kouzes and Posner echoed that sentiment when they wrote,

> Leaders we admire...do not focus on satisfying their own aims and desires; they look for ways to respond to the needs and interests of their constituents. They are not self-centered; they concentrate on the constituent.[248]

Their emphasis here is on "leaders we admire." Certainly there is nothing new to what they wrote. All leaders at one time have been followers, and each knows what they liked and disliked in leaders they served. Naturally if current leaders respected and worked harder for those past leaders who they saw concentrate on the needs of the followers, then the current leaders should do the same.

There is an important aspect, though, to the idea of taking care of one's people and seeing to their needs, and it underlies the concept of servant leadership in general. That is, leaders must look to the needs and desires of those they lead, but this does not by any means imply that the leader is merely a waiter or valet to those whom they serve, catering to their followers' each and every whim. The leader must more importantly know what their followers need and not just what they want. The most telling illustration of this is when Christ washed the feet of his disciples.

> The evening meal was being served, and the devil had already prompted Judas Iscariot, son of Simon, to betray Jesus. Jesus knew that the Father had put all things under his power, and that he had come from God and was returning to God; so he got up from the meal, took off his outer clothing, and wrapped a towel around his waist. After that, he poured water into a basin and began to wash his disciples' feet, drying them with the towel that was wrapped around him. He came to Simon Peter, who said to him, "Lord, are you going to wash my feet?" Jesus replied, "You do not realize what I am doing, but later you will understand." "No," said Peter, "you shall never wash my feet." Jesus answered, "Unless I wash your feet, you have no part with me." "Then, Lord," Simon Peter replied, "not just my feet but my hands and head as well!" Jesus answered, "A person who has had a bath needs only to wash his feet; his whole body is clean…Now that I, your Lord and Teacher, have washed your feet, you also should wash one another's feet. I have set you an example that you should do as I have done for you" (John 13: 2-10, 14-15, NIV).[249]

There are a few items aspiring leaders should take note of here about Christ's style of leadership. First, verse 3 states that Christ knew the Father had put all things in his power and that he was from and going back to the Father; in other words, Christ was secure and confident in himself and did not do this act out of a sense of insecurity or weakness. Christ never took on this task because he felt he was the least valued and therefore was the one who had to do it. He acted from strength.

Second, he put the needs of his disciples first. He got up and washed his disciples' feet while "the evening meal was being served." He put his hunger and his own needs behind him until he could properly care for his twelve companions.

Third, Christ did not cater to his disciples, but gave them what they needed. At first, Peter did not want his feet washed, but instead of giving in to Peter's idea of what he needed Christ told him what he really did need. Then, when Peter wanted more, Christ told Peter that what he had was sufficient. Christ saw to their needs, not to their wants.

The Blackabys stated about Christ's relationship with his disciples,

> Christlike servant leaders must understand whom they serve…
> Spiritual leaders are not their people's servants; they are God's…
> Jesus wasn't trying to give his followers what they wanted; he
> was determined to give them what his Father wanted to give
> them…Jesus was his Father's servant, not theirs. Even as Jesus
> served his disciples, there was no question in anyone's mind
> that he was still their Lord.[250]

This is an excellent point. Christ served his disciples according to their needs, and in doing so never abdicated his leadership.

The same is true of military leadership. Leaders in the military are responsible for taking care of their people but also accomplishing the mission, sometimes preparing for war and sometimes fighting a war. These are by no means pleasant tasks. The US Army teaches its leaders this important point:

> Taking care of soldiers means creating a disciplined
> environment where they can learn and grow. It means holding
> them to high standards, training them to do their jobs so
> they can function in peace and win in war. You take care of
> soldiers when you treat them fairly, refuse to cut corners, share
> their hardships, and set the example. Taking care of soldiers
> encompasses everything from making sure a soldier has time
> for an annual dental exam to visiting off-post housing to make
> sure it's adequate…It doesn't mean coddling them or making
> training easy or comfortable. In fact, that kind of training can
> get soldiers killed. Training must be rigorous and as much like
> combat as is possible while being safe. Hard training is one
> way of preparing soldiers for the rigors of combat. Take care of
> soldiers by giving them the training, equipment, and support
> they need to keep them alive in combat.[251]

Colonel Meyer used another term, compassion, for the idea of servant leadership. This compassion, he wrote, is not just a suggestion; it is completely necessary.

> You gotta have compassion. Compassion is absolutely essential for a leader. Compassion doesn't mean you're weak. It means you're sympathetic—fair—to your soldiers when you should be. Command is tough, and you gotta be tough, but you can't be unmoved by your soldiers' problems…The 'gut-most' important point is you have to care for your company and your troops! You must be sincere and willing to go that extra mile for your soldiers. Soldiers can distinguish a 'ticket punching,' insincere commander from one who wants to command for all the right reasons. Only grudgingly do they follow a commander who's just going through the motions of command.[252]

This compassion is not difficult to have when the leader truly values his people and treats them as more than just as tools or expendable material used to get a job done. The Blackabys were correct when they stated,

> Servant leadership flows from the love leaders have for their people…Leaders who equate bottom-line results with success are sadly deluded. When a company accomplishes its goals but decimates the lives of its members, it may win the battle but lose the war.[253]

It is interesting to note, too, how being valued is what people want most and what inspires them most to work for a leader. An interesting analysis of this phenomenon came from US Navy Captain D. Michael Abrashoff who related how he faced plummeting morale when he took command of the USS *Benfold*. He wrote of the experience:

Pondering all this in the context of my post as the new captain of *Benfold*, I read some exit surveys, interviews conducted by the military to find out why people are leaving. I assumed that low pay would be the first reason, but in fact it was fifth. The top reason was not being treated with respect or dignity; second was being prevented from making an impact on the organization; third, not being listened to; and fourth, not being rewarded with more responsibility. Talk about an eye-opener.[254]

Taking Captain Abrashoff's experience as an example, there are a few things followers look for from a leader. The first, Captain Abrashoff discovered, was respect, and his experience was not by any means isolated. Retired US Air Force (Reserve) Major General William A. Cohen found similar results and wrote,

> Ninety percent of leaders I have surveyed put job security, high pay, and good benefits in the top five [motivators]. That is, they think that these factors are the most important to their employees. But these three factors are usually far down the list.[255]

If job security, high pay and good benefits were not what motivated people, then what, according to Major General Cohen, did? Perhaps not surprisingly, "Work with people who treat me with respect" was ranked number one.[256] If a leader respects and values those that work for him, his own leadership gains respect in return. Larry Michael wrote, "Competence in leadership also depends on one's skills and abilities in relating to people. People buy into you before they buy into your leadership."[257]

Kouzes and Posner wrote similarly that the credibility followers ascribe to their leaders is directly related to how much the leader values his people as people, and not just as workers. They wrote,

> The secret to closing the credibility gap lies in a collective willingness to get closer, to become known, and to get to know others – as human beings, not as voting statistics or employee numbers. By getting closer to their constituents and by letting their constituents get to know them, leaders can strengthen their foundation of credibility.[258]

This knowing goes far beyond just an introductory handshake. Leaders must truly seek to understand who their followers are and what drives them. One mistake leaders make is to assume that their followers will open up and tell the leader what their concerns are. In fact, the opposite is true; followers generally won't offer feedback. Leaders need to solicit input from their followers. Kouzes and Posner continued,

> Being able to build relationships starts by learning how to understand and see things from another's perspective...The greater the extent to which we comprehend each other's perceptions, concerns, and values, the greater our ability to work together...So, as leaders, we must not simply articulate our own philosophies. We must learn to listen to others.[259]

This input must also be a dialogue. As Colonel Meyer cautioned, "Don't be a know-it-all. Being a know-it-all is the quickest way to shut off communication. Instead, you want your soldiers to open up and tell you what they think."[260]

This need for dialogue also shows how suggestion boxes and various other tools have limited value. Real feedback, through dialogue, can only come through contact—personal and sincere contact. Kouzes and Posner stated clearly,

> Listening can't be achieved from a distance, by reading reports, or by hearing something secondhand…Since proximity is the single best predictor of whether two people will talk to one another, we have to get close to people if we're going to communicate. And since most of our constituents cannot come to us, we have to go to them.[261]

Kouzes and Posner also state that when a leader asks for feedback, the leader must also be willing to accept feedback in the form of criticism. Even the best of leaders will frequently make mistakes and subordinates must be free to point them out when necessary. "Leaders demonstrate that they value others," they wrote, "when they listen to them, trust them, and are receptive to having others point out their own mistakes or other problems."[262] When the leader is the proverbial emperor with no clothes on, his people must be free to point it out without fear of retribution. This again hearkens back to the need for humility in a leader.

A leader shows he values his followers by acknowledging their contributions to the efforts. If one remembers that humility is an essential part of effective leadership, then Rick Bereit's words will resonate: The opposite of humility is not pride, it's ungratefulness."[263] Indeed, when a leader only values his own contribution in the success of an organization or fails to see the contributions of others, his leadership will suffer. Abraham Zaleznik suggested along those same lines, "A leader is more interested in what events and decisions mean to people than his own role in getting things accomplished."[264] Leaders need to keep this in perspective: No leader can succeed without the success of the followers as well. "Leaders ought to be constantly praising their people for their accomplishments and acknowledge their contributions to the organization," wrote the Blackabys. "Fact is, when people are successful, so is the leader."[265]

Leaders must also show how they value their subordinates by giving up some of their leadership to them and allowing them to make an impact through leadership and initiative of their own. Again, a leader's own insecurity and lack of humility often get in the way of allowing others to grow as leaders. "Credible leaders" wrote Kouzes and Posner, "are not afraid to liberate the leader in everyone."[266] Allowing a person to take the lead within an organization shows value through trust.

It seems like a risk to stray from the traditional formula of dictatorial and forceful leadership and instead turn to servanthood as a means of leadership, yet it is a risk worth taking. When leaders sacrifice their personal prestige and instead practice leadership through serving, they find they have far more effectiveness, and hence far more prestige, than they would have otherwise. It is not really a radical thought. As Kouzes and Posner wrote, "The concept of servant leadership is not new. Nearly twenty years ago, Robert Greenleaf pointed out that 'the great leader is seen as a servant first, and that simple fact is the key to [the leader's] greatness.'"[267] The result of sacrificing prestige is greatness, not loss of it.

One result of servant leadership which a leader must have in order to be effective is a greater sense of loyalty. People speak of demanding loyalty, and yet this is impossible; leaders can demand obedience but never loyalty. "Do you understand," wrote Colonel Meyer, "that loyalty is a two-way street?"[268] The leader must show loyalty first, but when he does he will earn it in return. "Loyalty," wrote Kouzes and Posner, "is not something a leader can demand. It is something the people – the constituency – choose to grant to a leader who has earned it."[269]

The same is true with respect. As with loyalty, "Leaders cannot demand respect. They can only earn it."[270] Yet when a leader starts by showing respect to his subordinates, respect for them as people and respect for what contributions they make to the organization, they will find the respect returned. At least two of the greatest leaders in Scripture illustrate this concept. "Like Joshua," wrote the Blackabys, "Samuel refused to demand respect from the people, and, like Joshua, he was greatly venerated."[271]

Taking the time to know and truly understand one's followers may also strike traditionalists as risking a leader's "image" as a leader. This may be true, but as a leader allows the "image" to melt away by knowing his people and treating them with kindness and respect, the leader will gain even greater followership. "We will work harder and more effectively for people we like,' wrote Kouzes and Posner. "And we will like them in direct proportion to how they make us feel."[272] When a leader drops the image of the distant leader and takes the time to know his people, he will not need to demand loyalty; his people will freely give it. As Kouzes and Posner wrote, "People willingly follow the direction of someone who is attuned to their aims and aspirations, worries and fears, ideals and images."[273]

Kouzes and Posner also make an interesting connection:

> Leaders must make certain that other people's highest priority needs are being taken care of first. They must ask whether those being served are growing – becoming healthier, wiser, freer, more autonomous, more capable – and are more likely themselves to become servant leaders.[274]

By setting the example of a servant leader, a leader is more likely to create servant leaders among his subordinates. When subordinate leaders see the example of the organizational leader, they too will be more likely to adopt the same principles. The Blackabys point out,

> Spiritual leaders ought to serve their people. But their acts of service should be motivated and directed by the Holy Spirit. When leaders are not afraid to roll up their sleeves and serve their people, they encourage a corporate culture in which people willingly serve on another. When people serve each other ungrudgingly, they forge a unity that enables their organization to accomplish far more than if individuals worked on their own. Servanthood breaks down barriers and eliminates turf wars.[275]

And what leader doesn't want unity or a lack of barriers and turf wars among his followers? Servant leadership, when demonstrated at the top and taken on by others in the organization, will bring a cohesion and level of cooperation in the unit which can never be dictated or mandated through a policy letter. It can only be demonstrated.

When a leader sacrifices his own prestige by sacrificing power and credit, the leader can and will bring out the latent leadership in his followers. Captain Abrashoff testified to how that happened on board the USS *Benfold* and throughout his career in the Navy.

> My years in the Navy taught me that the art of leadership lies in simple things – commonsense actions that ensure high morale and increase the odds of winning…Leaders must be willing to put the ship's performance ahead of their egos, which for some people is harder than for others. The command-and-control approach is far from the most efficient way to tap people's intelligence and skills. To the contrary, I found that the more control I gave up, the more command I got.[276]

And yet again, what leader does not want more command – more influence – over his subordinates? By shunning the old "command and control approach" and allowing his subordinates to show initiative and display their own skills, he got far more done than he could have on his own. All leaders can put this principle to work.

A leader must sacrifice prestige and his own ego in order to be effective as a leader, especially as one called by the Holy Spirit. Yet the lesson through Scripture, as well as through experience, is that the more the leader is willing to sacrifice, the more he will get in return. Leaders must turn away from consolidating power and demanding respect and loyalty, and instead start giving it. As Rick Bereit wrote to military leaders,

> Jesus told his disciples that the power-wielding, abusive leadership they were used to was not part of God's plan. In His plan for godly leadership, those who served would become the great ones…As we carefully consider his command and His example, it's easy to see the merit in the method. A leader who extracts performance by force and positional power achieves, at best, exactly what he asks for and no more. A leader who guides with wisdom, while looking out for the needs of his people, will be surprised at the levels of performance subordinates achieve. A selfless leader earns trust from his followers.[277]

Ultimately, when applied to leadership, Christ's words in Scripture prove themselves true: "Whoever exalts himself will be humbled, and who humbles himself will be exalted" (Matthew 23:12, NKJV).[278]

CHAPTER 11
Sacrifice Of Personal Ambition

Paul wrote to the Philippian Christians a warning: "Do nothing out of selfish ambition or vain conceit" (Philippians 2:3-4, NIV).[279] This is a command which applies to leadership probably more than any other discipline. Traditionally leaders have been known to be ambitious, people who set their sights on personal achievement and go after it. In the past, this may have been considered virtuous, but today it is seen that way much less. As Kouzes and Posner wrote,

> Another significant change is in the value of being ambitious. In 1987, 21 percent selected it as an admired leadership quality; in our most recent study, only 10 percent did. Maybe the message is finally getting through that a self-serving style is no longer so beneficial to success in organizations as once thought.[280]

In the military, ambition is everywhere. People strive to make rank and take on greater responsibility. Higher rank seems to equate to more success, and lack of rank seems to indicate one is not a successful leader. The military's "up or out" philosophy, where one is separated or forced to retire if one doesn't get promoted, probably exacerbates what is already a negative trend. While nobody will criticize mission accomplishment, missions are frequently accomplished for the wrong reasons and at the expense of those of lower rank. Former Secretary of the Air Force Sheila Widnall spoke of it:

> Examples of careerism and self-interest are present at every level, but they do the most damage when they are displayed by the leader. If the leader is unwilling to sacrifice personal goals

for the good of the unit, it's hard to convince other members of the unit to do so. At that point the mission suffers, and the ripple effects can be devastating.[281]

This is not confined to the military. Even among Christian organizations where self-sacrifice is a known virtue, selfish ambition is evident among many leaders. The Blackabys wrote, "The sad truth is that many Christian organizations and churches are led by people who sought an office for all the wrong reasons. These people directly associated the size of their ministry with their own self-worth."[282] It is interesting that leadership of a larger church or ministry is to pastors what rank and command size is to military members; neither being in charge of a large church or large squadron is at all wrong, but too many leaders aspire to them for their own self-interest and glorification. In seeing this problem, Bishop Steven Neill went so far as to say, "To tell a man he is called to be a leader is the best way of ensuring his spiritual ruin, since in the Christian world ambition is more deadly than any other sin, and, if yielded to, makes a man unprofitable in the ministry."[283]

Selfish ambition is a poison that will kill any organization. Sanders asked mournfully, "Has not ambition caused the downfall of several otherwise great leaders in the church, people who fell victim to the 'last infirmity of noble minds'?"[284] It is human nature, perhaps to want more—more status, more power, more accolades, more accomplishments—yet when such ambition is simply for personal gain, it can be destructive not only to the leader but for the followers who are left behind in the rubble.

It is not that promotion or moving on to greater responsibilities are evil or sinful, nor is the desire for these things inherently wrong. However, when this becomes one's greatest motivation, over service to one's country, service to one's organization, or doing the will of God, it becomes a destructive force. Bereit noted,

> Promotion and pay are important aspects of all work. When you pursue them in a balanced way, you will find contentment and fulfillment. If you make them your main focus, you will lose your joy and feel like you never have enough.[285]

Christ's words are well-known: "No one can serve two masters; for either he will hate the one and love the other, or else he will be loyal to one and despise the other" (Matthew 6:24, NKJV),[286] or as Eugene Peterson wrote it, "You can't worship two gods at once. Loving one god, you'll end up hating the other. Adoration of one feeds contempt for the other" (Matthew 6:24, *The Message*).[287] Certainly this is true: How many ambitious leaders become angry with God when they are not able to fulfill their ambitions or get the promotions they feel they deserve? Yet leaders do not have the luxury of dabbling between God's plan and one's ambitious desires since it is the followers who ultimately suffer for a leader's failures. Leaders are called to choose between ambition and fulfilling the calling of the Holy Spirit: "Choose for yourselves this day whom you will serve" (Joshua 24:15, NKJV).[288] "Spiritual leaders understand," wrote the Blackabys, "they cannot relentlessly pursue their own personal goals and glorify God at the same time."[289]

Selfish ambition is just that—selfish. "Make no mistake about it," wrote Rick Bereit. "The source of evil that flows from our minds, mouths, and actions is our own heart."[290] Indeed, selfish ambition is "evil" as Bereit says, and this evil cannot co-exist with a heart that yearns to follow the Holy Spirit.

Colonel Meyer asked a question of aspiring Army officers, and this is one every aspiring leader needs to answer: "Are you willing to sacrifice your career to protect and preserve the dignity of your soldiers?"[291] A leader's whole reason for being a leader is for the well-being of the organization and its people, and for a leader called by the Holy Spirit it is also to fulfill the Holy Spirit's call. If a person is not willing to sacrifice his career for these things, he ought not aspire to be a leader because he will not be an effective one. Leadership requires a sacrifice of personal ambition.

This does not mean that all ambition is bad. Many confuse the meaning of Jeremiah 45 which speaks about ambition. Oswald Sanders clarified,

> And so Jeremiah gave Baruch some very wise and simple counsel: 'Should you then seek great things for yourself? Seek them not' (Jeremiah 45:5). The prophet was not condemning all ambition as sinful, but he was pointing to selfish motivation that makes ambition wrong – 'great things for *yourself.*' Desiring to be great is not a sin. It is motivation that determines ambition's character. Our Lord never taught against the urge to high achievement, but He did expose and condemn unworthy motivation.[292]

There are, in truth, noble ambitions. One which is applicable for all leaders which cannot be overstated is the ambition to seek and follow God fully. "Let him who boasts boast about this: that he understands and knows me...for in [this] I delight" (Jeremiah 9:24, NIV).[293]

The Apostle Paul was an ambitious person when it came to opening up new territory for spreading the Gospel. "It has always been my ambition," he wrote to the Christians in Rome, "to preach the Gospel where Christ was not known, so that I would not be building on someone else's foundation" (Romans 15:20, NIV).[294] Ambitions through which leaders intend to glorify God are noble ambitions.

Even in such areas as business, ambition is not inherently sinful. James counseled fellow believers about how to distinguish good ambition from bad as they planned their business ventures:

> What causes fights and quarrels among you? Don't they come from your desires that battle within you? You want something but don't get it. You kill and covet, but you cannot have what you want. You quarrel and fight. You do not have, because you do not ask God. When you ask, you do not receive because you ask with the wrong motives that you may spend what you get on your pleasures…Now listen you who say, "Today or tomorrow we will go to this or that city, spend a year there, carry on business and make money." Why, you don't even know what will happen tomorrow. What is your life? You are a mist that appears for a little while and then vanishes. Instead, you ought to say, "If it is the Lord's will, we will live and do this or that" (James 4:1-3, 13-15, NIV).[295]

What this passage tells the ambitious person is that it is by no means wrong to set goals, but that one must consider three things: 1) That the goal is not for "selfish pleasures"; 2) that the goal is considered in light of eternity, since our lives are brief and essentially meaningless on their own; and 3) that we look to see if what we intend to do is consistent with God's will. These can even apply to goals that a leader sets in the military: A military leader should ask, "Is the goal simply for my good and to make me look good or for the good of the unit? Is the goal going to have a lasting impact, or am I just filling a square? Is what I am doing glorifying God?" Military leaders who build their ambitions and goals around these questions need not fear that they are following selfish ambition. If a military leader shuns selfish ambition but works hard for the good of the unit, he will achieve excellent ambitions. As Sanders wrote, "When our motives are right, this work [leadership] pays eternal dividends."[296] Putting God and one's followers before oneself is critical, and it is effective. As Sanders also wrote, "Ambition that centers on the glory of God and welfare of the church [or

Washington and Sacrifice
Studying the life of George Washington, I see that there really are two phases of his life. First, there was Washington, the shameless self-promoter. Washington was intent on climbing the social ladder, and the only way he could achieve that was through military advancement. In his early years he flattered and almost pandered to those who could get him the military leadership positions he wanted even though his abilities proved greatly lacking. However, there seems to be a shift later in his life, which was marked by sacrifice. He knew that accepting the role of commander-in-chief of the Continental Army would be an immediate death sentence if the struggle for independence failed. Even if they were successful , Washington would not personally benefit from it, since he requested to be able to serve without pay (how many generals would do that today?). The effort to lead a rag-tag army against the world's best army took its toll on him physically, and he greatly aged in the process almost to the point of losing his vision. Yet his leadership by sacrifice – demonstrated by his donning of his spectacles as he spoke with them to make up for his failing eyesight – is what ultimately convinced his officers from rebelling against the Continental Congress when their pay was long overdue, far more than any logic or moving speeches ever could have. Had he been the self-promoter now as he had been in the past he could never have convinced his officers to remain patient and continue to work without pay, but because he had personally sacrificed so much, putting the needs of his country and of his army ahead of his own well-being, they continued following his example.

of any followership body] is a mighty force for good."[297] Putting God's will ahead of our own is also necessary. In developing their goals and ambitions, leaders must first turn to God for guidance. As the Blackabys wrote, "There is nothing a leader can do that will guarantee God's affirmation. All a leader can do is submit. Some spiritual leaders try to be more committed. What they need is to be more submitted."[298] Yet, when a leader places his will second to God's will, God is faithful in return. S. D. Gordon once commented, "Let it once be fixed that a man's ambition is to fit into God's plan for him, and he has a North Star ever in sight to guide him steadily over any sea, however shoreless it seems."[299]

There is advice in the Gospel directed specifically at military members. As John the Baptist was preaching repentance and the coming of the Messiah, "some soldiers asked him, 'And what should we do?' and he replied, 'Don't extort money and don't accuse people falsely. Be content with your pay" (Luke 3:14, NIV).[300] This again is often misconstrued; it doesn't imply that a member of the military, especially a leader, is following God's will by stagnating professionally or otherwise. Rick Bereit wrote, "Contentment does not mean you shouldn't mature, improve, and be promoted."[301] Growing as a leader and improving one's skills are excellent ambitions, and when they result in promotion a leader has a good reason to sense some satisfaction. Yet a leader must be careful that when he is growing and improving he is doing so as a leader and military professional, and not as a salesman. Promotion is admirable; self-promotion is not. "The true spiritual leader," wrote Sanders, "will never campaign for promotion."[302] And as Bereit wrote,

If you're content with your pay, does this mean you will end up as a 'one striper' or a lieutenant? If you have no desire to advance, won't you end up on the bottom rung? Both logic and experience say, 'No.' Promotion in the military is not based on your ability to sell yourself. It's based on demonstrated ability to perform at the next highest rank.[303]

Therefore, leaders must put selfish ambitionaside and focus only on ambition which is not self-oriented, which reaches for long-term and eternal goals, and which glorifies God.

To a degree, this may sound like a leap of faith with all of the comfort Peter might have had stepping out of the boat onto the water. And yet, those who willingly sacrifice personal ambition to follow God's call to them as leaders will find that God is trustworthy. Leaders who sacrifice themselves and their ambitions can trust God with the results. These leaders will find success.

When we say this, we have to know what success means. To those called by the Holy Spirit, success is, as the Blackabys wrote:

> God gauges success in terms of faithfulness and obedience, not in terms of dollars or status. The definitive measure of a leader's success is whether they moved their people from where they were to where God wanted them to be. This may be reflected in numbers, or even in financial growth, but it is expressly seen in the spiritual growth of the followers. The measure of a leader's success is whether or not they accomplished God's will.[304]

Following God's lead does not at all mean that we are neglecting the mission of the organizations we serve. Military leaders need to prepare their units for combat and business leaders need to ensure a profit; without these accomplishments, leaders will not remain in leadership positions very long regardless of how many "souls they have saved." But all leaders in whatever role they find themselves must put God's calling first. When they do, God is faithful to bring them the material or tangible successes they need.

In fact, these other successes, such as military successes, are just as spiritual as evangelism or discipleship when God uses them to validate one's spiritual leadership and bring himself glory. For instance, God told Joshua prior to the attack on Jericho, "Today I will begin to exalt you in the eyes of all Israel, so that they may know that I am with you as I was with Moses" (Joshua 3:7, NIV).[305] While a military victory may not seem spiritual, God worked mightily through Joshua as a military leader in order that Joshua might also become the spiritual leader for Israel that Moses had been. Gideon was also such a case. God brought him a spectacular military victory in order to glorify himself; and he made it even more spectacular to ensure he received the glory, for he told Gideon,

> You have too many men for me to deliver Midian into their hands. In order that Israel may not boast against me that her own strength has saved her, announce now to the people, "Anyone who trembles with fear may turn back and leave Mount Gilead." So, twenty-two thousand men left, while ten thousand remained (Judges 7:2-3, NIV).[306]

God brought Gideon a military victory, and in doing so glorified himself. When God does such things as well, he will remember to honor those who faithfully serve him. The Blackabys explain the secret of Joshua's success:

> Joshua had not embarked on a quest for military glory and fame. God gave it to him. Joshua owed every achievement and victory to God. Joshua's success as a leader clearly came from God. God was the one with the ability. Joshua's part was to live in obedience to God. The lesson for leaders is obvious: spiritual success is not defined in terms of ability – it is a matter of obedience.[307]

Self-promotion, even in spiritual matters, is never becoming a leader chosen by God. Christ spoke of such people when he said,

> Be careful not to do your "acts of righteousness" before men, to be seen by them. If you do, you will have no reward from

your Father in heaven. So when you give to the needy, do not announce it with trumpets, as the hypocrites do in the synagogue and on the streets, to be honored by men. I tell you the truth, they have received their reward in full...And when you pray, do not be like the hypocrites for they love to pray standing in the synagogues and on the street corners to be seen by men. I tell you the truth, they have received their reward in full (Matthew 6: 1-2, 5, NIV).[308]

When leaders, especially those in the military, do their work "to be seen by men" or "to be honored by men," they may indeed achieve the promotion or honor they want. But that is all they will get. As the Blackabys said,

Jesus never promoted himself, even when Satan tried to entice him to do so. This is the pattern of true spiritual leadership. When spiritual leaders pursue the praise and respect of others, they may achieve their goal, but they also have their reward in full. Some people solicit awards, positions, and honors from others. If they succeed, they will be esteemed but their honor will come from people, not God. Those who seek God's affirmation receive a true and lasting honor. There is no comparison between the fleeting praise of people and the esteem of God.[309]

So is a military leader sacrificing chances at promotion by not being a "square filler" or by not taking credit for everything his unit accomplishes? By no means; Scripture ensures us that to do such things is hardly a recipe for promotion, and neither is refusing to do them professional suicide. Asaph wrote in the psalm, "For exaltation [promotion] comes from neither the east, nor from the west, nor from the south. But God is the judge. He puts one down and exalts [promotes] the other" (Psalm 75:6-7, NKJV).[310] Solomon said the same when he wrote, "The king's heart is in the hand of Yahweh, like the rivers of water; He turns it wherever he wishes" (Proverbs 21: 1, NKJV).[311] "Proverbs 21:1," wrote Bereit, "reminds us that it is easy for Him to move the 'king's' heart—that applies to military supervisors and promotion boards as well."[312] Certainly as a sovereign God, Yahweh can and will dictate to promotion boards who He determines deserves the promotions. A leader who is faithful to the calling of the Holy Spirit need never fear a promotion board.

Leadership is sacrifice. There is no other alternative. When one is called to leadership, he can expect to be required to sacrifice of himself—sometimes even suffering is the lot of leadership—and sacrifice of his own prestige, as well as putting his own ambition aside for the sake of the call of the Holy Spirit.

While this sounds dire, and it is by no means ever easy—it can be stressful, lonely, painful, and frustrating—we are assured that the God who calls leaders to serve is a faithful God. When leaders put their organizations and their people ahead of themselves, taking on the role of a servant, and treat their subordinates with respect and dignity, they will find they get it in return. When a leader puts God's plans ahead of his own and stops seeking selfish ambition, God is strong enough to reward those who faithfully seek him.

When a leader makes these sacrifices to please the one who has called him, though it may cost him dearly, God has promised, "Those who honor me, I will honor" (1 Samuel 2:30, NIV).[313]

PART IV
Six Biblical Qualities Of Leaders

Opinions about what a leader should be or do are as numerous and varied as the number of people who ponder the question. Certainly, what qualities are considered necessary also depend on the situations or contexts in which leaders find themselves; warrior leaders may need some different qualities than corporate leaders and ecclesiastical leaders may need different qualities than political leaders. However, Biblical research reveals at least six qualities which also figure prominently in many secular and military studies on leadership. These qualities are strong families, competence, vision, wisdom-based decision-making, courage, and integrity. A person called by the Holy Spirit to serve as a leader must possess and maintain these as foundational for leadership success. The need for these qualities in military leaders is especially acute.

CHAPTER 12
Family

Stating that a strong family is necessary for a leader may seem unusual. Few leadership books discuss this. Indeed, most do not even mention families at all. This should not imply that a leader cannot be effective if unmarried, but for those who are married it is very clear that a leader must have strong family support if he or she expects to be effective on the job. At the same time the leader must ensure his or her family is a top priority, even ahead of a Holy Spirit-energized leadership role.

This is not, nor has it ever been, an easy balance for a leader to maintain, especially for a leader in the military. Civil War historian James McPherson stated that this was a common struggle for both Union and Confederate soldiers as they went off to fight. For the soldiers who served, simply deciding whether or not to serve put a strain on their families well before facing any hostilities. Many men volunteered as a matter of honor and duty, whether because one believed in the cause of the nation he served or because he could not bear the stigma of cowardice for failing to go forward. Yet this very decision to fight for one side or the other was the cause of strife and division within many of the soldiers' families. As McPherson wrote, "Honor was primarily a masculine concept, not always appreciated by wives who sometimes felt that a man's duty to his family was more important than pride in his reputation."[314] Even from the very beginning, soldiers' families had to make sacrifices with the husbands and fathers gone. They had to endure the long separations and carry on the work the men would have been doing in their homes were they present. They had to suffer as well if the men returned injured or did not return at all. The specters of death and danger hung over the families' heads as much as they did the soldiers'.

McPherson stated, though, that without the willingness of the families to endure the hardships, the soldiers would have been far less effective on the battlefield. The very thought that they may have lacked the support of home often undermined all of the other motivations that drove the men to serve and be brave. This was true in both armies in the 1860s, and it continues to be true in recent times. McPherson explained,

> Convictions of duty, honor, patriotism, and ideology functioned as the principle sustaining motivations of Civil War soldiers, while the impulses of courage, self-respect, and group cohesion were the main sources of combat motivation. But without a firm base of support in the homes and communities from which these citizen soldiers came, their morale would have crumbled. Even the solidarity with comrades in arms was insufficient to sustain their commitment if it lacked sustenance on the home front. In the Vietnam War the erosion of that sustenance was one reason for a decline in the motivation and fighting power of the American army.[315]

Undoubtedly, the willingness of soldiers to endure the hardships of combat depended heavily on what kind of support they felt they were getting from home. This has also been true, and continues to be true, for leaders in the military. Even more than the average soldier, the military leaders must know they have the support and backing of their family members in spite of the sacrifices and hardships they mutually endure if they expect to be effective as leaders. Colonel John G. Meyer, Jr. (US Army, Retired) asked aspiring company commanders a number of questions to help them determine if they are fit for command. One very straightforward question was, "Is your family willing to bear the sacrifices?"[316] The importance of this question lies in his previous question to these junior officers, "Are you willing to dedicate yourself 24 hours a day, seven days a week, if necessary, for your unit and your soldiers?"[317] Leadership and command by their very nature are demanding roles, and no one who is unwilling to invest the time or make those sacrifices should assume that role, and consequently no one whose family will not support him and share in those sacrifices hould aspire to that role.

Most leaders will probably concede that they need strong families at home backing them up, but there is a strong possibility that few understand their own role in keeping their families strong. The truth is, leaders cannot neglect their families and still expect them to thrive and offer support to them as they lead. A significant insight into this comes from Paul's letter to Timothy, where he describes the qualifications of leaders in the church. Godly leaders, stated Paul, must first and continually demonstrate their

An Inappropriate Relationship
As I was beginning my first squadron command, a seasoned colonel gave a classroom full of us new commanders some interesting words of wisdom. "Command," he said, "is a very jealous mistress." It was amazing how this man could compare such an awesome thing like commanding a squadron to committing adultery, but it proved to be very true. Being a leader demands your time, thought, and energy, leaving you with very little to bring home to your family, and the more you succumb to its demands the less it leaves you to bring home. But by recognizing it for what it is, a leader can put this mistress in her proper place. There will be times when our families need to do without us, there will be some late nights at the office, and there are frequent moments when they won't have our complete attention, but leaders need to learn that not every office emergency is a real emergency, and that there are times you need to shut off the mobile phone. As long as you jump every time your mistress calls, you will sacrifice your family even more.

leadership at home. A leader, he wrote,

…must be blameless, the husband of one wife…one who rules his own house well, having his children in submission with all reverence (for if a man does not know how to rule his own house well, how will he take care of the church of God?). (1 Timothy 3:2, 4-5, NKJV)[318]

Eugene Peterson's paraphrase, *The Message*, adds poignancy to this qualification. He wrote,

If anyone wants to provide leadership in the church, good! But there are preconditions. A leader must be well-thought-of, *committed to his wife*…He must handle his own affairs well, attentive to his own children and having their respect. For if someone is unable to handle his own affairs, how can he take care of God's church? [Emphasis mine] (1 Timothy 3:1-2, 4-5, *The Message*)[319]

A leader must not only have an orderly home at face value, but must be completely and unconditionally committed to his wife. Likewise, any leader knows that he cannot earn the respect of his followers if he neglects them, and it is no different when he is supposed to be the leader in his own family. He must earn the respect of his children by loving them, being attentive to them and seeing to their needs. He must also lead them spiritually; as Larry Michael wrote, "The leader should set the example of devotion and prayer in the home."[320] There is no doubt that strife at home will negatively impact a leader's effectiveness in the organization. Richard and Henry Blackaby warn those who put their ministry or business first,

> Every leader must balance the responsibilities of their leadership role with the commitment to their families. Those who wholly sacrifice their families may achieve great success in the public eye but privately suffer tremendous personal turmoil.[321]

Yet even more to the point, when Paul asks whether a leader can be a leader for God if he cannot handle his own house, he is hardly being rhetorical. He is not asking Timothy to ponder a parallel between styles and types of leadership, he is actually asking a fundamental question. He is asking how a man can effectively lead in the church or in any area to which he is called by the Holy Spirit when he is neglecting his own family and opening it up to strife; a leader who does so is personally undermining the very support which is so indispensable to him as a leader! Leaders cripple themselves when they put their calling to leadership ahead of their leadership role within their families. Oswald Sanders wrote of this,

> The Christian leader who is married must demonstrate the ability to "manage his own family well and see that his children obey him with proper respect" (1Timothy 3:4). We cannot accept the picture of a stern, unsmiling patriarch, immune to laughter and impervious to emotion. But Paul urges a well-ordered home where mutual respect and supportive harmony are the keynotes. Failure to keep home in order has kept many [leaders] from their fullest potential.[322]

This is where some leaders find themselves struggling. They feel called to service as a leader by the Holy Spirit and justify the sacrifice of their families for the sake of this calling. This is especially amazing since God made it quite clear that service to one's country, however noble it may be, must be secondary to his role in the family. For this reason, God commanded the Israelites, "When a man has taken a new wife, he shall not go out to war or be charged with any business; he shall be free at home for one year, and bring happiness to the wife whom he has taken" (Deuteronomy 24: 5, NJKV).[323] Certainly, there will come a time for every leader when his family will have to sacrifice to support the leader's calling, but each must ensure he has established a firm foundation for his family first. As Matthew Henry wrote of this commandment,

> Provision made for the preservation and confirmation of love

between newly married people. This rightly follows the laws concerning divorce, which would be prevented if their affection to each other was well established at first. If the husband was away from is wife much the first year, his love for her would be in danger of cooling...therefore his service to his country in war, embassies, or other public business that would call him from home, shall be dispensed with.[324]

So clearly, a leader is called to be both the leader in his calling and a leader at home. In order to be effective in both, the leader must prioritize by putting his family first. He cannot expect success by blending the two; as Rick Bereit stated, "It is important for the parent who is in the military to distinguish family life from military life."[325] Indeed, the leader must make a distinction and put his family in top priority. Sanders wrote,

> While a leader is caring for church and mission, he must not neglect the family, which is his primary and personal responsibility. The discharge of one duty in God's kingdom does not excuse us from another. There is time for every legitimate duty.[326]

Joshua was a prime example of this sort of leadership. He knew full well the calling he had to lead Israel and that his call came from Yahweh himself, and yet he still put his role as a leader in his family first. John Maxwell pointed out,

> As a leader, where should your influence begin? A good example can be drawn from the life of Joshua. For him – as for other leaders wanting to make an impact beyond their lifetimes – it began at home. Before anything else, Joshua took responsibility for the spiritual life of his family.[327]

Interestingly, though, Maxwell pointed out that, while Joshua put his family leadership first his national leadership did not suffer. In fact, it thrived because he prioritized this way. He wrote,

> It may sound ironic, but when a leader puts his family first, the community benefits. When a leader puts the community first, both his family and the community suffer. Starting at home is always the key to affecting others in a positive way. Because Joshua had his priorities right, and had led his household well, he gained credibility to lead the entire house of Israel.[328]

This should actually be no surprise to any leader called by God. Moses clearly stated that God blesses those who put him first in their priorities. "Keep his decrees and commands, which I am giving you today," Moses wrote, "so that it may go well with you and your children after you and that you may live long in the land the Lord your God gives you for all time" (Deuteronomy 4:40, NIV).[329] When people follow God's priorities, he blesses them in return; and God's priorities for his leaders are clear. Larry Michael wrote,

> The Christian leader's first priority is not to himself; his primary commitment is to Christ. He must lay himself at the altar before God and deny himself in following Christ. His next priority is to the persons whom God has placed under his roof. He has a unique role of providing godly leadership to the people closest to him—his own family. Yes, many demands outside the home are placed on a leader, but he has to make a choice. The right choice is to prioritize his commitment to his family. God has placed him as the head of his home, and he must assume that spiritual responsibility and the practical functions of it.[330]

Clearly, then, prioritization of leadership obligations leads to success. Putting the family first will lead to success in the leadership role the Holy Spirit has called people to outside the home, but it is just as clear that this is not true in reverse. Michael wrote well,

> The manner in which a man leads in his home has direct implications on how he will lead in his work. If he succeeds at home first, that success will undergird his work at the office or on the job. If he fails with his family, he ultimately will fail in his all-encompassing role as a leader. All of the success in the world cannot replace what a leader loses when he fails in the primary responsibility of leading his family.[331]

This should be of great comfort to those called by the Holy Spirit to lead in the military. Military leadership is difficult and demanding; it requires great sacrifice by both the leader and the leader's family. It may seem impossible to handle both at times, yet such a leader will succeed when he puts the military second to his family.

CHAPTER 13
Competence

There was a Charlie Brown comic strip in which Charlie Brown bemoans his baseball team's inability to win by pondering, "How can we lose when we are so sincere?" Unfortunately, sincerity and good intentions cannot make up for poor performance, especially where leadership is concerned. Nor can faith, while certainly necessary, be a substitute for competence in a leader. An ineffective leader cannot long remain a leader; in spite of whatever other assets a leader has he will be ineffective if he is incompetent. As Leroy Eims stated, "Good intentions can't replace good performance. Leaders must be competent in the job God has given them to do."[332] God expects excellence in the leaders he has chosen, and so do the leaders' followers.

This is probably more true for leaders than for those with any other spiritual gift. Is not competence something we demand in our leaders? Of course it is. As Kouzes and Posner wrote, "If we are to enlist in another's cause, we must see the person as capable and effective."[333] Likewise, if we presume to lead, we should assume our followers expect the same of us, and how much more so in the military! According to the US Army leadership manual,

> "The American soldier...demands professional competence in his leaders," General Omar Bradley said. And this is true not only in the Army but everywhere in the public, private, and nonprofit sectors. People willingly follow only those who know what they are doing. One of the quickest ways for a leader to lose the trust and commitment of followers is to demonstrate incompetence.[334]

Not only will incompetence cause a leader to lose the trust and commitment of followers, but it can also be deadly. This is why Brigadier General Malham Wakin (USAF, Retired) said that in the military competence means more than just achieving goals. Where combat and death are the lot of the military members, competence is a moral responsibility. He wrote,

> Is professional competence a moral obligation? It is not immoral under normal circumstances to fail a course in school. If a military person is incapable of learning to deal appropriately with a sophisticated weapons system, that is not immoral. But the leader who knowingly assigns the incapable to equipment they cannot operate is not merely foolish; where the stakes are so high in terms of the survival of society, loss of human life, and use of national treasure, it seems clear he has entered the moral realm. With respect to the development of tactics, weaponry, long-range strategy, and the conditions for employing those weapons systems which pose serious threats to noncombatants, the military leader's competence is a crucial issue. Literally, he has a moral obligation to be competent in these areas.[335]

Colonel Meyer was equally as blunt in his writing to junior officers. He said simply: "You gotta be competent. Technical and tactical proficiency are musts. Your soldiers look to you for answers and solutions. You must produce."[336]

This, too, is where some Christian military leaders may find a stumbling block when they perceive that as long as they focus purely on spiritual disciplines, their leadership qualities will take care of themselves. True, the Holy Spirit can be more active through a leader if he does devote himself to spiritual disciplines, but a leader's influence will suffer if he is not competent. As much as it is necessary for a leader called by the Holy Spirit to devote himself to prayer and seeking God, these cannot be his only activities. A leader must also strive for excellence in his area of expertise and as a leader. As Rick Bereit wrote, "Zeal for the Lord should not detract from your ability to serve with excellence. On the contrary, your work as a Christian should reflect the high standards you have learned from following Jesus."[337] The pursuit of holiness is not an excuse for substandard work, and especially not so coming from the leader who is supposed to be a model for the organization. Larry Michael suggests that spiritual disciplines and professional skill go hand in hand, and both must be continually increased. Without them, the leader's other skills will fall short. He wrote,

> The leader today must be committed to competence. Education, personal charisma, and natural abilities might achieve a short-lived following, but there is no substitute for the continued development of spiritual gifts and practical skills.[338]

Even gifts and talents given by God are insufficient when left unattended. Leaders must fully develop the gifts and talents they have. Wayne Grudem wrote, "Even though we are given gifts by God, we are still responsible to use them effectively, and to seek to grow in their use."[339] Indeed there may be a thought that because one has a spiritual gift then one can solely rely on God for its use, but those with spiritual gifts cannot see themselves merely as passive players in the use of these gifts. Those gifted with leadership must work to develop and sustain this gift.

There is no doubt that any ability left unattended can lose its effectiveness. Kouzes and Posner wrote, "Left unattended, knowledge and skill, like all assets, depreciate in value – surprisingly quickly."[340] But amazingly, this is not only true of one's personal abilities but of even of spiritual gifts. There is evidence in Scripture which indicates that spiritual gifts may fall into decay if not exercised and developed. Grudem stated of this,

> "I remind you to rekindle the gift of God that is within you (2 Tim 1:6)." It was possible for Timothy to allow his gift to weaken, apparently through infrequent use, and Paul reminds him to stir it up by using it and thereby strengthening it. This should not be surprising, for we realize that many gifts increase in strength and effectiveness as they are used.[341]

Additionally, while it may be taken for granted that a leader has a certain expertise in the area in which he leads, he cannot be an effective leader without continually improving on the skills he possesses. A leader must seek out opportunities to grow and strengthen what he has. "To strengthen credibility," wrote Kouzes and Posner, "you must continuously improve your existing abilities and learn new ones. And that takes time and attention."[342] The US Army agrees with this philosophy, and states, "Good leaders make it a regular practice to add to their knowledge and skills. They seek out mentors, opportunities to learn, and challenges that will make them grow."[343]

As Kouzes and Posner stressed one's technical skill, so Oswald Sanders stressed improving one's mental qualities. He wrote, "Spiritual leaders should also read for intellectual growth. This will require books that test wits, provide fresh ideas, challenge assumptions and probe complexities."[344]

Sanders also pointed out that part of competence is a constant re-evaluation of oneself and one's skills. He wrote, "The first step toward improvement is to recognize weaknesses, make corrections, and cultivate strengths."[345]

Skills required of a leader must continually be broadened, not allowed to remain narrow. The US Army states that there are four "key skills" every leader must have. Leaders, according to the US Army, must have interpersonal skills which include coaching, teaching, counseling motivating, and empowering individuals, and team building. Leaders must also have conceptual skills, which include creative, analytical, and ethical thinking and sound judgment. They must also have technical skills, which are the job-related skills. They must also have tactical skills, by which the US Army means is the ability to solve problems in order to achieve the objective.[346] Whether in the military or in a ministry, all leaders should seek to develop competence in these areas.

In essence, then, a leader must be competent, yet never complacent. Leaders must possess, develop, maintain, and improve the skills which may indeed be God-given, but which will suffer if neglected. If the leader allows these skills to suffer, then he will cripple his own leadership and ultimately damage his organization.

CHAPTER 14
Vision

One of the most important qualities of leadership in any context, be it military leadership, business leadership, or ministry leadership, is the ability of the leader to find and pursue a vision of where he wants the organization to go. With a vision, the leader determines the direction and the desired end state of the organization and in doing so can prioritize resources and time. Without a vision, the leader and the members of the organization may be very busy and work hard but will in the end accomplish very little. To be blunt, a leader himself is pointless if he is without a vision of where the organization is to go.

This is true of leadership in any context. A vision is the spirit of a person's leadership, without which all of the other qualities are lifeless. As Bill Hybels wrote,

> Vision is the very core of leadership. Take vision away from a leader and you cut out his or her heart. Vision is the fuel leaders run on. It's the energy that creates action. It's the fire that ignites the passion of followers. It's the clear call that sustains focused effort year after year, decade after decade, as people offer consistent and sacrificial service to God.[347]

Indeed, vision is the essence of the leader's being. If the leader has no vision – no picture of the future of his organization – then the leader will have no idea where he is going, and therefore will be unable to get there; this will make it especially difficult for him to inspire his followers to join him in the journey. If this is so, then the leader's ability to lead is ineffective from the very beginning. Kouzes and Posner wrote of this,

> We expect our leaders to have a sense of direction and a concern

for the future of the organization. Leaders must know where they are going...If leaders are to be admired and respected, they must have the ability to see across the horizon of time and imagine what might be. We are not inclined to follow those who are directionless.[348]

If this is so in any organization, it is especially true in the military where strong leadership can be the difference between success and failure in times of conflict or even in preparation for times of conflict. This is what also makes the difference between a true commander and an officer who may just be in the role to "fill the square"; the commander who understands the need for leadership will establish a vision and follow it through to completion. US Air Force Colonel David L. Goldfein, former commander of the 31st Fighter Wing and 52d Fighter Wing, wrote to new commanders,

You were not hired to 'tread water' in command. Rather, you are expected to move your squadron in a direction that more effectively accomplishes the unit's mission. This is true regardless of whether you are taking charge of a top-notch squadron or one that's on its back. Even the very best organizations can and will improve under the leadership of an inspirational commander. Developing a clear vision and then communicating that vision effectively are essential elements of successful commands.[349]

His brother, US Air Force Colonel Steve Goldfein, who commanded the 1st Fighter Wing, echoed those sentiments when he stated,

In the end, commanders do only two things – provide the vision and set the environment. Almost everything you do for the organization falls into one of these categories. You will be tempted to focus elsewhere. If you do so, it is likely you are performing someone else's job and they neither want nor need your help.[350]

Establishing and carrying out a vision is what separates true leaders from those who just occupy the position, and it is also one of the elements which separate leaders from managers. Certainly, good managers are essential to an organization, but without visionary leadership an organization will ultimately just be a group of people keeping busy for the sake of being busy and earning a paycheck, which is hardly inspirational to anyone.

Kouzes and Posner made that point clear: "We know from our research," they testified, "that being forward-looking is the quality that distinguishes leaders from other credible people."[351] People in an organization like good management, but they yearn for good leadership.

It is the visionary leader, not the manager, who thinks beyond what is and considers what can be. This again is where leadership is so essential and where there must be an understanding of the difference between management and leadership. Managers, by their very nature, do not establish a vision for the organization. US Navy Captain D. Michael Abrashoff wrote in order to make the difference clear,

> Management committees always want to see the metrics before they allow you to launch new ideas. Since, by definition, new ideas don't have metrics, the result is that great ideas tend to be stillborn in major companies today.[352]

So not only are leadership and management not synonymous, but they often work at odds against each other. Managers are masters of what is, and leaders are the makers of what can be. When the conflict arises, the leader must ultimately lead. As former Chairman of the Joint Chiefs of Staff and former Secretary of State General Colin Powell remarked, "Leaders have the ability to inspire others to achieve what managers say is not feasible."[353]

If leadership by its very definition requires vision, then one may well ask, "Where does this vision come from?" Unfortunately for many organizations, some leaders derive their vision from inappropriate sources. Some leaders equate "vision" with "targets of opportunity" or "low-hanging fruit"; they focus only on what an organization can do quickly and neglect what the organization should focus on in the long-term. This is not true vision for a leader, and neither does it inspire the followers. The Blackabys wrote of this kind of vision, "While it is one thing for people to risk their lives in pursuit of a dream, it is quite another for leaders to take their organizations on a misguided and unnecessary quest just because the opportunity lies before them."[354] The nature of leadership is sacrifice, certainly, but followers also make sacrifices for the fulfillment of the vision. Solo visionaries like George Leigh Mallory may be able to draw inspiration for feats such as climbing Mount Everest "because it's there"[355] and, like Mallory, will gladly allow their corpses to be the monuments to their efforts, but no leader has a right to ask his followers to sacrifice themselves for such a shallow reason. Followers want and deserve more.

Sadly but just as truly, many leaders derive a vision from their own personal desires and ambitions. The Blackabys wrote of this kind of leadership,

Although it is not always readily apparent, vanity is a source of vision that motivates many leaders. Some leaders set the goals for their organizations based on what will bring them the most personal success or praise…Such ego-centric leadership is generally cloaked in statements of loyalty to the organization or in pious proclamations about the kingdom of God… Napoleon Bonaparte was constantly involved in warfare as he led the French Empire in its attempt to conquer Europe. In defeat, Napoleon surmised, "If I had succeeded, I should have been the greatest man known to history." There is not doubt that Napoleon made a name for himself in history, but it's questionable whether his soldiers would have willingly sacrificed their lives on the battlefields of Europe had they known the primary cause was to secure their Emperor's fame. Today, many are called upon to make sacrifices and to give their best efforts on behalf of their organizations, but they do so with nagging doubts that their personal sacri ices are for no more noble purpose that furthering their leader's career.[356]

Sanders, 56.

When this sort of leadership evolves, the leader is essentially asking the organization to work and sacrifice purely for his own advancement, and this is hardly inspirational or motivating to the followers. Many leaders may even think they are aiming for altruistic goals when in reality they are looking to their own needs, so a leader must have the wisdom to check his own motives frequently to ensure he is not attempting to fool himself as well as his followers. A leader must look beyond himself when he establishes a vision for the organization.

One place a leader can and should look in order to establish a vision for his organization is to his superiors. This can mean instructions, regulations, or established standards put in place by a higher headquarters, service, or next echelon of authority. It could also mean the leader's own boss or commander. In the military, every commander answers to another commander. When in command, a leader should find out what his own commander wants to achieve within the larger organization and determine how his own unit fits into that larger vision. Biblically, this is appropriate. Christians find in Scripture the command to do the bidding of the one to whom one answers, and this does not exempt those who are leaders in their own right. A commander must execute the orders and mission of his own commander. While people today do not like to equate themselves to

---

My Plan

While commanding a squadron in Germany, I developed a very ambitious plan for increasing our fighting effectiveness as a unit. It was a combination of intense training, a reorganization of our personnel, and a new shift schedule which would allow us to train without sacrificing any of our shiftworkers time off. I was excited about it and planned it down to the detail. When I presented it to the squadron I didn't get the real buy-in that I wanted, so I chalked it up to the inevitable inertia that goes along with any change. During my time there, I was able to accomplish some of what I had planned but not all of it, and I left wondering why it really didn't catch on even though most of my people would readily admit it was the right thing to do. It wasn't until later that I realized my failure in executing my plan – it was my plan. I had developed it and I had imposed it. Even though it was a good enough plan, few people bought into it because they didn't have any ownership of it. In retrospect, I should have presented what I wanted to see happen – better training without sacrificing time off – and let them come up with how to do it. If I had done that, then my junior officers and senior NCOs would have been implementing what they came up with, not with what was only *my* plan.

---

slaves of two thousand years ago, the principle Paul wrote of was the same:

> Slaves, obey your earthly masters with respect and fear. Obey them not only to win their favor when their eye is on you, but like slaves of Christ, doing the will of God from your heart. Serve wholeheartedly, as if you were serving the Lord, not men, because you know that the Lord will reward everyone for whatever good he does, whether he is slave or free.[357]

So, whether one is a new private, seaman recruit, or Airman Basic, or whether one is a seasoned commander of a unit, one must look to his own commander to know what one should achieve for himself and for those in his charge.

This is important as well for another reason in addition to finding a vision for the organization: If leaders are expected to "make disciples" of those whom they lead, there is nothing which indicates in Scripture that a leader cannot also "make disciples" of his superiors in the same way. This is exactly what Eugene Peterson indicates in his paraphrase of the same passage:

> Servants, respectfully obey your earthly masters but always

with an eye to obeying the real master, Christ. Don't just do what you have to do to get by, but work heartily, as Christ's servants doing what God wants you to do. And work with a smile on your face, always keeping in mind that no matter who happens to be giving the orders, you're really serving God. Good work will get you good pay from the master, regardless of whether you are slave or free.[358]

Clearly, those called by the Holy Spirit to lead a military organization will fulfill the Great Commission by following his commander with just as much dedication as he would expect of those in his own unit.

There are very solid Biblical examples of leaders who lead by following the lead of those over them. Joseph is a prime example. No matter what situation he was in, he served his own leaders to the fullest and in turn became an effective leader. One example is his service to Potiphar:

Now Joseph had been taken down to Egypt. And Potiphar, an officer of Pharaoh, captain of the guard, an Egyptian, bought him from the Ishmaelites who had taken him down there. The LORD was with Joseph, and he was a successful man; and he was in the house of his master the Egyptian. And his master saw that the LORD made all he did to prosper in his hand. So Joseph found favor in his sight, and served him. Then he made him overseer of, and all that he had put under his authority. So it was, from the time that he had made him overseer of his house and all that he had, that the LORD blessed the Egyptian's house for Joseph's sake; and the blessing of the LORD was on all that he had in the house and in the field. Thus he left all that he had in Joseph's hand, and he did not know what he had except for the bread which he ate.[359]

Joseph served a leader, the captain of Pharaoh's guard, and served him faithfully. In turn, Potiphar appointed Joseph to be the leader of his household. Joseph was completely successful, and Potiphar recognized Yahweh as the source of Joseph's capabilities. Joseph led those of Potiphar's house by being a faithful follower of his own superior, and God received the glory for it.

As events unfolded, Joseph found himself unfairly put in prison. While no one could blame him if he had become cynical or reclusive, Joseph chose to continue to be a leader where he was by carrying out his superior's orders.

Then Joseph's master took him and put him into the prison, a place where the king's prisoners were confined. And he was there in the prison. But the LORD was with Joseph and showed him mercy, and He gave him favor in the sight of the keeper of the prison. And the keeper of the prison committed to Joseph's hand all the prisoners who were in the prison; whatever they did there, it was his doing. The keeper of the prison did not look into anything that was under Joseph's authority, because the LORD was with him; and whatever he did the LORD made it prosper.[360]

Again, Joseph did not lead from selfish ambition but as a faithful follower of his superior. Joseph succeeded as a leader again but this time he did so in a situation which would have been a challenge to the best of leaders; he was in charge of fellow prisoners who either were people of less-than-desirable character and motives, or people who, like Joseph, had a good reason to be bitter. In either case, Joseph was in charge of people who were probably not very highly motivated or willing followers. Yet he succeeded. Because Joseph was faithful to his own boss, Yahweh made him prosper.

This rule applies even when a leader is subordinate to someone who perhaps is self-serving or an undesirable leader. A leader called by God does not have the luxury or discretion to ignore his own leader's vision, unless that vision involves illegal or immoral actions. An example of a leader who served a bad superior is David in the service of Saul. Jealous of David's success as a subordinate leader, Saul made several attempts to kill David; sadly, Saul was not the model of the inspirational and empowering leader every follower deserves. But David in turn served Saul faithfully all the more. On one occasion, David evaded Saul's deadly grasp but assured Saul he would still be a faithful follower:

> Know and see that there is neither evil nor rebellion in my hand, and I have not sinned against you. Yet you hunt my life to take it. Let the LORD judge between you and me, and let the LORD avenge me on you. But my hand shall not be against you. As the proverb of the ancients says, "Wickedness proceeds from the wicked." But my hand shall not be against you....Therefore, let the LORD be judge, and judge between you and me, and see and plead my case, and deliver me out of your hand.[361]

David here was hardly a sycophant who would quickly excuse Saul's poor behavior; neither, though, did he excuse himself from service to Saul in spite of this somewhat extreme personality conflict. David could have led his followers on a course apart from Saul or even against him, but instead David continued to lead his followers in faithful service to their God-anointed king.

Scripture insists that each be a faithful servant and follow the lead of those over us. Jesus himself made that point to his opposition, as recorded in Matthew 22:

> Then the Pharisees went out and laid plans to trap him in his words. They sent their disciples to him along with the Herodians. "Teacher," they said, 'we know you are a man of integrity and that you teach the way of God in accordance to the truth. You aren't swayed by men, because you pay no attention to who they are. Tell us then, what is your opinion? Is it right to pay taxes to Caesar or not?" But Jesus, knowing their evil intent, said, "You hypocrites, why are you trying to trap me? Show me the coin used for paying the tax." They brought him a denarius, and he asked them, "Whose portrait is this? And whose inscription?" "Caesar's," they replied. Then he said to them, "Give to Caesar what is Caesar's, and to God what is God's." (Matthew 22: 15-21, NIV)[362]

As with Saul, Caesar was not really the picture of servant leadership, yet Christ did not excuse his followers from lawfully following the commands of Caesar. If Caesar legally demanded taxes, Christ's followers were to pay them; if Caesar demanded respect, Christ's followers were to give it; if Caesar demanded service, Christ's followers were to do so faithfully. Even a leader who serves a poor leader must lead his unit in achieving his leader's vision.

This same passage, however, gives the follower of Christ yet another source from which to derive the vision which is so crucial to leadership. While we must "render unto Caesar" our faithful service, we will also "render unto God." If we can look to the authority over us for vision, we can also look to the God who called us to leadership for vision. This is not only what a leader called by the Holy Spirit can do, it is what the leader called by the Holy Spirit should do. The Blackabys explain,

> Too often, people assume that along with the role of leader comes the responsibility of determining what should be done.

They develop aggressive goals. They dream grandiose dreams. They cast grand visions. Then they pray and ask God to join them in their agenda and to bless their efforts. That is not what spiritual leaders do. Spiritual leaders seek God's will, whether it is for their church or for their corporation, and then they marshal their people to pursue God's plan. The key to spiritual leadership, then, is for spiritual leaders to understand God's will for them and for their organizations. Leaders then move people away from their own agendas and on to God's. It sounds simple enough, but the truth is that many Christian leaders fail to put this basic truth into practice. Too often leaders allow secular models of leadership to corrupt the straightforward model set forth by Jesus...Jesus did not develop a plan nor did he cast the vision. He sought to do his Father's will. Jesus had a plan for Himself and for his disciples, but the vision came from his Father.[363]

It is a common occurrence, yet odd when one thinks about it, that a leader may know the Holy Spirit's calling to him to be a leader yet then assumes that he must then derive a vision solely by himself. Logic should tell us that if the Holy Spirit calls someone to leadership, then it is because the Holy Spirit has a purpose to fulfill. Would not then the Holy Spirit reveal that purpose to the leader or would the Holy Spirit allow that leader to flounder, find his own way, or simply pursue his own goals? It is silly to think that the God who called us to leadership will not also set a vision for us, and it is even sillier to substitute our own visions in the place of his. "Every time leaders choose to develop their own vision for their people instead of seeking God's will," wrote the Blackabys, "they are giving their people their best thinking instead of God's. That is a poor exchange indeed."[364]

God's vision should always take primacy, if not be exclusive, over our own. Larry Michael wrote, "A visionary leader is positive about the future because God has given a vision of that future."[365] This also stands to reason. We as leaders do not control the future, nor do we know it. However, the God who commissioned his leaders does indeed know and mold the future. If this is so, does it not make logical sense to adopt the vision of the one who knows the future than to rely on ourselves who are blind to it? Following God's vision always provides a reason for optimism for success which exceeds that which we can derive on our own. "Wise leaders," wrote the Blackabys, "recognize that life is far too complex to comprehend apart from God's revelation and guidance."[366]

As stated in a previous chapter, God's vision may be temporal or it may be spiritual, or indeed it may be both. The Holy Spirit places leaders in positions of leadership in all areas, military and civilian, to achieve his purposes. Leaders find that when they follow the Holy Spirit's lead and vision, they will find temporal success that help fulfill the Holy Spirit's desires. The Blackabys wrote of this phenomenon,

> Spiritual leaders should be motivated by the Holy Spirit. As Henry [Blackaby] regularly consults with Christian CEOs, it is startling what they share God is revealing to them about his purposes. Corporate CEOs are finding that when they meet with world leaders, they are not only able to transact multimillion-dollar business deals, but also to give their witness for Christ.[367]

In Psalm 25, David wrote of this phenomenon where a person goes about ordinary daily business in the fear of Yahweh, and in the midst of this business—even if the activity not inherently spiritual in nature—Yahweh reveals deeper plans to the faithful follower.

> Who, then, is the man that fears the LORD? He will instruct him in the way chosen for him. He will spend his days in prosperity, And his descendents will inherit the land. The LORD confides in those who fear Him; He makes His covenant known to them. (Psalm 25: 12-14, NIV)[368]

God keeps leaders in all areas and, whether it be transacting multimillion-dollar business deals, planning a church social, or attacking an enemy, when the leader is committed to serving God in that capacity, God will reveal his eternal plans to that leader at just the right time. When the Lord is ready, he will "instruct" and "confide" his plans to the leader for him to carry out.

How does a leader receive this vision from the Holy Spirit? If adopting the Holy Spirit's vision is essential to the leader's success, the leader must be able to answer this question.

The first thing every leader must do in order to understand the Holy Spirit's vision for his leadership is to commit himself to submitting to that vision. Using Abraham as an example, the Blackabys wrote, "The key was not for God to bless Abraham's plans but for Abraham to discard his agenda in favor of God's will."[369] The leader, while being able to have additional goals or visions, must put these behind those of the Holy Spirit.

The leader, too, must seek the vision of the Holy Spirit. This is difficult for many leaders to do, as the Blackabys explained:

> Too often Christian leaders operate under a false sense of assurance that they are seeking God's will. Being proactive by nature, leaders want to rush into action. As a result, they don't spend enough time seeking to hear clearly from God. Instead, they simply have a cursory moment of prayer and then begin making their plans.[370]

Truly, leaders by nature are people of action; they thrive on getting things done. Yet before a leader called by the Holy Spirit can go into action, he must stop and earnestly seek what action the Holy Spirit has in mind. Only then will the Holy Spirit impart his vision to the leader.

When a leader does consult the Holy Spirit, seeking his guidance, and when he does submit to the Holy Spirits agenda, he must also do another thing: He must give the Holy Spirit the room to work and not confine him to a preconceived idea. The Blackabys make a fascinating point about God's work throughout Scripture. Leaders, they wrote:

> ...should take careful note that, throughout Scripture, God rarely worked in the same way twice. God's activity was always unique to the people with whom he was dealing and the time in which he was working. God's activity cannot be reduced to a formula because God is always more concerned with peoples' obedient response to his will than with the means of communicating that will. Churches are remiss if they assume that because God worked mightily in a particular way in the past, he will choose do work in exactly the same way in the present. Many organizations today are locked into doing things a certain way, not because it is still effective, but because it was effective yesterday. This is the curse of success.[371]

While it is always advisable to study the successes and failures around us, we cannot and must not confine the Holy Spirit to working within these parameters. Yet all of the scheming and studying by human leaders, however wise, cannot possibly replace the specific direction of the Holy Spirit. The Blackabys wrote,

> In the case of churches emulating the success of other

churches, it seemingly eliminates the need for Christian leaders to cultivate an intimate relationship with God. While there is nothing wrong with churches making use of successful programs and methods developed by others when they sense God has led them to use them, church leaders can be seduced into thinking all they need to lead their church is the latest seminar or popular book. They spend their energy chasing after whatever new program or fad gains their attention. Such leaders spend too little time examining and evaluating the effectiveness of their own organizations and cultivating their relationship with the Head of the church while spending an inordinate amount of time focusing on the activities of others. Pity the people who follow such thoughtless leadership.[372]

For those who are brought to leadership by the Holy Spirit, then, it is not so much a human-conceived vision which a leader needs but more of a God-given revelation. Leaders must receive God's revelation before acting which is not easy for many, especially for those who want earnestly to do something for God. Their ambition is admirable, but sometimes misguided. The Blackabys made a great point when they wrote of such people who want to develop grand visions for God:

Many Christian leaders have adopted BHAGs (Big Hairy Audacious Goals) with gusto. Yet, at times there seems to be a hollowness to their rhetoric. They say, 'We need to dream big dreams for God,' or 'We must set goals that are worthy of the mighty God we serve.' This all sounds exciting and can generally elicit a chorus of amens from the audience, but is it biblical? Isaiah 55:8-9 cautions, '"For my thoughts are not your thoughts, neither are your ways my ways"' declares the LORD. "For as the heavens are higher than the earth, so are My ways higher than your ways and My thoughts your thoughts."' The message is clear. Leaders' best thinking will not build the kingdom of God. Why? Because people do not naturally think the way God does...He has different priorities, different values. When people think 'mighty thoughts for God' and 'dream great dreams for God,' the emphasis is on dreams and goals that originate from people rather than from God. The danger is in believing that human reasoning can build God's kingdom. It cannot...Ephesians 3:20 says, 'Now to him who is able to do immeasurably more than all we ask or imagine, according to his power that is at work within us.' This Scripture ought to motivate Christian leaders as they seek God's will for their organizations. How significant are Big Hairy Audacious Goals when viewed in light of this verse? Can leaders impress God with their grandiose visions? Is it possible for a leader to dream any dream which is worthy of God? Can even the most perceptive leader look into the future and determine what would be the most desirable outcome for their organizations to achieve? The Apostle Paul puts vision into its proper perspective. God remains unimpressed with leaders' grandiose schemes and dreams because he is able to do immeasurably more than mortals can comprehend. Spiritual leaders who develop their own visions, no matter how extensive, rather than understanding God's will, are settling for their best thinking instead of God's plans.[373]

As admirable and well-meaning as such planning is, it is most likely based on adrenaline and enthusiasm rather than on the Holy Spirit's guidance and strength. All leaders must resist coming up with Godly schemes and instead wait on God to reveal his vision to his leaders. Revelation and only revelation will result in doing the will of God and the calling of the Holy Spirit. This goes against the nature of most leaders and it certainly goes against worldly thinking. Leaders resist such an idea because they consider themselves as leaders to be the focal point of the effort, and any other focal point will reduce their status as leaders. But a leader called by the Holy Spirit must yield to the Holy Spirit's direction. The Blackabys wrote on this,

> The world functions by vision. But God does not ask his followers to operate by vision. God's people live by revelation …There is a significant difference between revelation and vision. Vision is something people produce; revelation is something people receive. Leaders can dream up a vision, but they cannot discover God's will. God must reveal it. The secular world ignores God's will, so nonbelievers are left with one alternative – to project their own visions. Christians are called to a totally different approach. For Christians, God alone sets the agenda.[374]

The leader, then, must assert his leadership in following out the Holy

Spirit's vision. "The role of spiritual leaders," wrote the Blackabys, "is not to dream up dreams for God but to be the vanguard for their people in understanding God's revelation."[375] The revelation of the Holy Spirit must come first, taking priority over those visions which the leader himself may formulate.

Leadership, however, does not end with receiving a revelation or developing a vision; this is just the beginning. Once a leader has the vision, he must then chart a course for completing the vision. "The competent leader," wrote Larry Michael, "is goal oriented, continuing to look to the future."[376] Goals chart a path to the fulfillment of the vision; if the leader does not know how to get there, neither can he lead his followers there.

As the leader is charting this course, he must remain optimistic. There will be obstacles to success, of course, but the leader who has a vision or revelation will know that there is a way to get through those obstacles and get the job done. Major General William Cohen (US Air Force, Retired) wrote of this optimism,

> All commandos have one common belief system: They believe there is always a way...When the need arises, don't focus on your problem. Instead, focus on the idea that there is always a way and start thinking about various possibilities.[377]

For the leader guided by the Holy Spirit, this is more than just feel-good cheerleading; this optimism is well-founded. Whether in the office or on the field of battle, military leaders can be confident that they will fulfill the vision if they trust in the God who gave them the role of leadership. As Moses told the Israelites,

> When you go to war against your enemies and see horses and chariots and an army greater than yours, do not be afraid of them, because the LORD your God, who brought you up out of Egypt, will be with you...Do not be fainthearted or afraid; do not be terrified or give way to panic before them. For the LORD your God is the one who goes with you to fight for you against your enemies to give you victory (Deuteronomy 20:1-4, NIV).[378]

The opposite, though, is also true. When a leader, however gifted, actively disobeys God's command or does not seek the Holy Spirit's guidance, he may very well lead his followers to disaster in spite of his natural attributes as a leader. Moses wrote of how the Israelites, accustomed to victory on the battlefield, went forward against the Amalekites and

Canaanites even though Moses advised them that God was not with them.

> Early the next morning they went up toward the high hill country. "We have sinned," they said. "We will go up to the place the LORD promised." But Moses said, "Why are you disobeying the LORD's command? This will not succeed! Do not go up, because the LORD is not with you. You will be defeated by your enemies, for the Amalekites and Canaanites will face you there. Because you have turned away from the LORD, he will not be with you and you will die by the sword." Nevertheless, in their presumption they went up toward the high hill country, though neither Moses nor the ark of the LORD's covenant moved from the camp. Then the Amalekites and Canaanites who lived in that hill country came down and attacked them and beat them all the way to Hormah" (Numbers 14: 40-45, NIV).[379]

Leaders must continually remember that God's calling is not license for the leader. Leaders will find great reason for optimism, but only when in the Lord's will.

Leaders must also know how to communicate the vision to the followers. After all, it is their role to execute the vision of the leader and they cannot do so unless they fully understand it and take ownership of it. Colonel David Goldfein wrote this advice to squadron commanders:

> Once you have developed your vision, you must then communicate it throughout your squadron. Take and make every opportunity to talk to your troops about your vision and their role in it. It should become the centerpiece of a "mini-speech" you give when meeting with members of the squadron. Repetition in the early months of your command is critical to ensuring that the word filters to all levels of the organization. When Ronald W. Reagan was president, he stuck to a few key themes throughout his eight years in office. As he constantly repeated these ideas, we came to understand more clearly the direction he intended to lead our nation. On a slightly smaller scale, you must do the same as commander of your squadron. By taking the time to first develop and then communicate your vision to the squadron, you will begin your command tour with a clear sense of direction and purpose.[380]

Colonel Goldfein is correct that repetition is the key to communicating the vision. It can not be a one-time statement. The commander must let the vision be a part of everything he does and make the vision a part of everything his subordinates do. It must be an integral part of who the leader is and what the members of the organization believe.

This is another area where some leaders misunderstand their roles. They think that communicating a vision means "selling" a vision. But this, as the Blackabys pointed out, is a mistake. Leaders called by the Holy Spirit should not have to sell the vision.

> In the Christian context, the process of selling a vision is flawed. If a vision must be sold to others, it is not a compelling vision and is probably not from God. Spiritual leaders don't sell vision; they share what God has revealed to them and trust that the Holy Spirit will confirm that same vision in the hearts of their people. Today, Christian leaders often develop a vision for their organizations and then demand the members either get on board or find another organization. This approach could not be further from the New Testament pattern. Spiritual leaders know they cannot change people; only the Holy Spirit can do this. If the Holy Spirit is not convincing people to follow in a new direction, it may be that God is not the author of the new direction.[381]

Christian leaders who have to rely on clever wording, salesmanship, or even trickery perhaps do not understand the role of the Holy Spirit. If the Holy Spirit gives the vision, the Holy Spirit does not need to rely on human wiles to get the point across. The leader should not have to sell the vision, just live it. A leader can inspire followers by living the vision, but even the best of salesmen who don't live the vision will be hollow leaders indeed and ultimately will inspire no one. As Bill Hybels wrote, "What good is a vision unless a leader can help others see it? But how? How does a leader best communicate a vision? By embodying it. By personifying it. By living it out."[382]

The leader must then do more than create a plan and inspire others; the leader must also carry it out. This may seem obvious but many leaders, particularly some who are considered great visionaries, "lack the skills needed to implement the vision"[383] according to Elmer Towns, Danny Lovett, and John Borek. Yet working the vision is just as essential as having the vision; a leader must bring the organization through the difficulties and resistance toward the end result. Larry Michael was correct when he wrote, "Leadership is the capacity to translate vision into reality. The vision means little if it does not result in implementation."[384] Or, to be even more to the point, as Kenneth Blanchard stated, "Good thoughts in your head not delivered mean squat."[385] Leadership involves vision, certainly, but carrying out the vision is an even more important aspect of leadership. Visions may come and visions may go, but those who achieve the vision are the only ones who deserve the title of leader. "Leaders who fix their gaze on the horizon, hoping for something better rather than focusing on the tasks at hand," wrote the Blackabys, "are unworthy to hold their current position."[386]

Yet when a leader has a vision, especially a Holy Spirit-inspired vision, develops a path to get there, lives it as his own, and perseveres to achieve it, he will find he has more than just an idea in his head. For one thing, a leader with a vision develops a passion for it. "First, a leader sees the vision, sees that life-changing image of the future that makes his or her pulse quicken," wrote Bill Hybels. "Then, almost immediately, comes the feeling of the vision…It's the energy and the passion it evokes deep in one's heart."[387] This passion is what drives a leader to succeed and inspires the followers to succeed. Vision-driven passion is contagious. Towns, Borek, and Lovett wrote,

> The same vision gives followers a dream to adopt as their own. It motivates people out of complacency to achieve what otherwise might be beyond them…it helps people endure the dark hours and difficult days they are bound to encounter in any leadership task.[388]

A vision inspires optimism. When people can see it, they are more apt to feel that they can achieve it as well. "Vision," wrote Oswald Sanders, "includes optimism and hope."[389] If this is so for any leader, how much more is it true for those whose vision came from the Holy Spirit? "True leaders understand," wrote the Blackabys, "that no matter how difficult the task before them, a group of people being led by the Holy Spirit can accomplish anything God asks of them."[390]

Such passionate and optimistic vision also yields one more benefit: They create a faith for future vision and revelation. It causes them to not only be receptive to more vision, but makes them seek it out as well. Kouzes and Posner wrote,

> Because of their faith, leaders are always searching, exploring,

and discovering what lies just beyond the horizon. Their strength is first of all an inner strength…it comes from knowing who they are, what they stand for, and where they are trying to go.[391]

This vision, given by the Holy Spirit and internalized and pursued by the leader, will result in passion, optimism and faith for the future. This is what Scripture requires in leaders.

CHAPTER 15
Wisdom-Based Decision-Making

"By definition," wrote Towns, Borek, and Lovett, "leaders are decision makers. You cannot lead if you will not decide."[392] They were completely correct: Leaders are decision-makers. There is and can be no question about this. The leader who cannot or will not make decisions is merely a figurehead or just incompetent. In any case, the indecisive leader may occupy a position of leadership but cannot effectively lead.

Effective leaders need to do even more; while they certainly should be able to reflect and think through problems, they also need to be able to make decisions quickly. As Sanders stated, "Swift and clear decision is the mark of a true leader."[393]

Biblically this is true as well. The best of leaders knew when they should ponder and dwell on a decision, but they could also act quickly when they needed to. Abraham was known more for being a patient, quiet, and persevering patriarch yet, as Sanders wrote, he "showed swift and clear decisiveness during the crisis at Sodom and the rescue of Lot…With great bravery he pursued the enemy and gained a victory over superior numbers."[394]

In the military, so Abraham demonstrated, decisive decision-making literally makes the difference between defeat and victory. In more recent times, General H. Norman Schwartzkopf personified a decisive leader, and he spoke of the need for decisive leaders.

> I think that throughout my early years in the army, I learned that probably the worst leader was one who wouldn't make a decision—I mean, who would just agonize over it, would never make a decision. A bad decision, at least, causes action to occur within an organization, and the organization itself can take a bad decision and turn around and make a good one. But

when you get no decision at all, then the whole organization just kind of sits there.[395]

Indeed, the US Army has also defined its leaders this way and has described its leaders in such a fashion:

> Infantry platoon and squad leaders must be tacticians. They cannot rely on a book to solve tactical problems. They must understand and use initiative in accomplishing the mission. This means that they must know how to analyze the situation quickly and make decisions rapidly in light of the commanders intent. They must be prepared to take independent action if necessary. The art of making sound decisions quickly lies in the knowledge of tactics, the estimate process, and platoon and squad techniques and procedures. The skills required of infantry leaders include physical toughness, technical knowledge, mental agility, and a firm grasp of how to motivate soldiers to fight in the face of adversity.[396]

Such decision-making, however, must be based on a solid foundation. Regardless of context, decisions made quickly and yet made out of anger, selfishness, faddish thinking or other such bases, can also lead to disaster. Indeed, there is a difference between making a decision quickly and making one in haste. Good leaders can make quick decisions because they already have a foundation from which to act. "Wisdom," as Sanders wrote, "gives a leader balance and helps to avoid eccentricity and extravagance."[397] Wisdom-based decision-making is the mark of a successful leader.

Admittedly, the concept of wisdom is difficult to precisely define as well, and an accurate picture of what wisdom-based decision-making is somewhat elusive. However, there are ways a leader can make good decisions quickly and at the same time guard him from "eccentricity and extravagance."

First, a leader must truly know what he is after. If he does not know what he is trying to achieve or where he is going, any decision he makes will be pointless. Major General Cohen remarked in that vein, "Having a clear and definite purpose is perhaps the most important principle of strategy, because you can't get there until you know where 'there' is!"[398]

This sounds like common sense; so it is, and sometimes common sense is also what should drive a leader in making decisions. Captain Abrashoff wrote of common sense in decision-making:

> How do you define the right thing? As US Supreme Court

justice Potter Stewart said about pornography, you know it when you see it. If it feels right, smells right, tastes right, it's almost surely the right thing – and you will be on the right track. If that doesn't sound very profound or sophisticated, in the Navy, in business, and in life, it really is as simple as that.[399]

All leaders know how to use past experience as well. While some leaders are perhaps more gifted than others, all must grow and mature, using experience as the most effective teacher. Biblically, this is sound. Towns, Borek, and Lovett used Joseph's mature leadership as such an example when they wrote, "Joseph did not learn to make decisions the day he was appointed to office by Pharaoh. He led by decision making through the varied experiences of his earlier life."[400] Colonel Goldfein pointed out that a leader should also rely on the experiences of others; quoting Martin Fanbee, he humorously wrote, "Learn from the mistakes of others. You won't live long enough to make them all yourself."[401]

Yet sometimes a decision is not quite so obvious. This is when a leader has to do research, or in a military context, gather intelligence. Major General Cohen explains why this is essential from a military perspective. He wrote,

> The basis of all strategy is to concentrate superior resources at the decisive point…Special operations theory differs in that it defies conventional thinking about what constitutes 'superior resources,' because on the battlefield, a small force is used to defeat a much larger or well-entrenched adversary…A small force can defeat an apparently stronger opponent only when the small force gains a decisive advantage over its adversary. [Navy Captain William H. McRaven] called this decisive advantage 'relative superiority' and stated that attaining it was essential for the success of any commando operation.[402]

This makes sense on the battlefield and it makes sense in the boardroom. With limited resources, a commander needs to know what the "decisive points" are in order to exploit them.

It may seem to many leaders that, being gifted by the Holy Spirit and given a vision from God, that they already have all of the information they need to make decisions, but precedent in Scripture shows that even the most Godly of leaders need to seek facts before they act. By looking a Gideon as an example, a leader can see how and why Gideon gathered intelligence prior to attacking the Midianites and Amalekites.

> It happened on the same night that the LORD said to him, "Arise, go down against the camp, for I have delivered it into your hand. But if you are afraid to go down, go down to the camp with Purah your servant, and you shall hear what they say; and afterward your hands shall be strengthened to go down against the camp." And he went down with Purah his servant to the outpost of the armed men who were in the camp. Now the Midianites and Amalekites, all the people of the East, were lying in the valley as numerous as locusts; and their camels were without number, as the sand by the seashore in multitude. And when Gideon, there was a man telling a dream to a companion. He said, "I have had a dream: To my surprise, a loaf of barley bread tumbled into the camp of Midian; it came to a tent and struck it so that it fell and overturned, and the tent collapsed." Then his companion answered and said, "This is nothing else but the sword of Gideon the son of Joash, a man of Israel! Into his hand God has delivered Midian and the whole camp." And so it was, when Gideon heard the telling of the dream and its interpretation, that he worshiped. He returned to the camp of Israel, and said, "Arise, for the LORD has delivered the camp of Midian into your hand" (Judges 7:9-15, NKJV).[403]

Leaders should note a few things about this story. First, Gideon had to gather the facts. Certainly, God promised Gideon the victory, but in this case God does not tell Gideon how to carry it out. Even in the case of Joshua at Jericho where God was fairly specific on how he wanted it done, Joshua still sent spies so he could have a better idea of what he was up against. "Although Joshua was confident of ultimate victory," wrote Towns, Borek, and Lovett, "he also recognized the need to gather intelligence."[404] Both, as good leaders, wanted as much information as they could get about their enemies. Second, Gideon planned the attack around the information he gathered. He knew he could not defeat the vast army of the Midianites and Amalekites with his small band of 300 if they fought man against man; but Gideon realized that his enemies were filled with fear. The attack he planned, then, was psychological; he used their fears against them and scared them into panic and retreat. This is exactly what

Major General Cohen meant when he wrote of "decisive points" and, as did Cohen's commandos, Gideon exploited those decisive points and beat his adversaries with a much smaller force. To find those points, he had to gather intelligence and facts.

Leaders called by the Holy Spirit have a great advantage over other leaders because they can ask of God. "If any of you lacks wisdom," wrote James, "let him ask of God , who give to all liberally and without reproach, and it will be given to him" (James 1:5, NKJV).[405] This is God's promise to any leader who finds himself in a situation where he finds his own wisdom is not equal to the situation – as if there is any leader who does not experience this. God alone is the source of wisdom for such people, and he gives it freely to those who ask. In fact, it should be comforting for leaders to know that when we look to God for wisdom he gives it without condemning or looking down on the one who asks. It is not that God is surprised when a leader turns to him for wisdom; it is to the contrary. God is just waiting for leaders to realize that for themselves. Solomon was an excellent example of a leader who realized his own inadequacy, refused to rely on his own wisdom, and threw himself on the mercy and wisdom of an all-knowing God.

> On that night, God appeared to Solomon and said to him, "Ask! What shall I give you?" And Solomon said to God: "You have shown great mercy to David my father, and have made me king in his place. Now, O Lord God, let Your promise to David my father be established for You have made me king over a people like the dust of the earth in multitude. Now give me wisdom and knowledge, that I may go out and come in before this people; for who can judge this great people of yours?" (2 Chronicles 1:7-10, NKJV)[406]

God called Solomon to be king over Israel, but not because Solomon inherently had all the answers. Indeed, God knew Solomon lacked ability and therefore required Solomon to ask of him. Only by doing so did God force Solomon to understand that God was really the source of his wisdom.

Matthew Henry made an interesting comment on this chapter. He wrote,

> God bade him ask what he would; not only that he might show him the right way of obtaining the favours that were intended for him, but that he might discover what was in his

heart. Men's characters appear in their choices and desires. *What would you have?* tests a man as much as *What would you do?* Like a genuine son of David, he chose spiritual blessings rather than temporal. His petition here is, *Give me wisdom and knowledge.* God gave the faculty of understanding, and to him we must apply for the furnishing of it…God gave him the wisdom that he asked for because he asked for it. God's grace shall never be lacking to those who sincerely desire to know and do their duty.[407]

Indeed, access to God's wisdom as a source from which we can make our own decisions is an advantage other leaders don't have. Even when a Godly leader has the experience, the intuition, and has gathered the necessary intelligence to make a solid decision, he should still seek of God and allow God's wisdom to take primacy over all other sources of wisdom.

As intuitive or experienced a leader may be, say the Blackabys, a leader must still consult with God to gain his insight. As they wrote,

> Spiritual leaders make two choices every time they make one decision. First, they choose whether to rely on their own insights or on God's wisdom in making their decisions. Their second choice is the conclusion they reach, or the action they take. People don't naturally do things God's way, because people don't think the way God does.[408]

In fact, Scripture makes it very clear that as wise or as intelligent a leader may be, he is still insufficient in his own to make the decisions necessary to please God. Proverbs 2 and 3 are replete about the need for a leader, or any person, to gain wisdom, and yet as John Maxwell states, "Proverbs 2 and 3 poses an apparent paradox in spiritual leadership. We are go get wisdom and understanding, yet we are not to lean on it apart from the Lord. Even good wisdom divorced from God can become a snare."[409] Indeed, a leader blessed with wisdom from God can miss the mark if he is not in tune with God's desires for that particular need and that particular moment, and if the leader does not consult with God every time he needs to make a decision he can fail miserably in spite of his many past successes. It is also tempting for leaders, looking back on these past successes, to think of themselves as the source of their own wisdom or to see themselves as beyond needing to call upon God for wisdom. This, says Matthew Henry, is exceptionally dangerous for even the best of leaders. "It is good to be wise," he wrote, "but it is bad to think of ourselves so; for there is more hope for a fool than for him who is wise in his own eyes."[410]

Even if a leader does recognize his need for proper input, he must know where his wisdom should come from. Certainly, many leaders understand the proverb, "Plans fail for lack of counsel, but with many advisers they succeed" (Proverbs 15:22, NIV),[411] but forget that God's wisdom is far superior and necessary yet. "When leaders are not oriented to God," wrote the Blackabys, "all their decisions – political, business and religious – are vulnerable to poor advice."[412] Rehoboam was a case in point. He sought counsel and received it from groups with various points of view – a commendable act for certain – but because he himself did not consult with Yahweh, he made a foolish decision which led to rebellion and a divided kingdom.

Sometimes as well, leaders need to go against the counsel of his advisors, and the leader who seeks and understands God's will can understand when he needs to do this, especially since going against the majority or popular opinion can put a leader at great risk. A leader cannot be bound to the advice of those around him, but needs to understand when to follow advice and when to decide alone. "A leader's decisions are not always based on the majority vote," wrote the Blackabys. "Spiritual statesmen are not driven by what people think but by what they know God has said. True spiritual leaders fear God far more than they fear people."[413]

In the same way that leaders need to know when counsel they receive is insufficient, so they must also know when current thinking is contrary to the guidance of the Holy Spirit. The military context may not seem to be the area in which "religious" or "spiritual" thoughts should be enacted, indeed the military lifestyle in general often appears to be completely godless, and yet in this context as well as any a leader needs to be able to shake off what passes for wisdom from those around him and seek God's guidance. "Spiritual leaders," wrote the Blackabys, "also allow the Holy Spirit to guide their thinking so that it is based on God's timeless truths rather than on society's latest fad."[414] Indeed, even quick decisions on the battlefield fall into the realm of these "timeless truths" of which the Blackabys speak, so every leader needs to allow God's wisdom to guide him through any decision.

And this is an excellent point for all leaders to remember, that ultimately it is God whom the leader is serving and it is always God's agenda that a leader must pursue. "Spiritual leaders make every decision with the awareness than one day they will give an account to God," wrote the Blackabys,[415] and there is much wisdom in this thought. Regardless of the environment to which the leader has been called to lead – military, business, ecumenical, political – everything the leader works for and every decision the leader makes is ultimately for God's glory. This thought should guide the leader in every decision he makes, especially when receiving counsel from those around him. "People-pleasing is not the driving force of spiritual leadership," wrote the Blackabys. "Spiritual leaders move people with them in their decisions but ultimately leaders are concerned about pleasing God, not people."[416]

So clearly, a leader needs to seek God in making any decision. Here too, though, the leader needs to be careful. If a leader must be able to make quick decisions based on the Lord's guidance, he must also be careful to avoid the "break glass in case of emergency" type of prayer. A leader should not expect Godly wisdom to permeate his own decision-making if he does not seek this wisdom regularly; God is not bound to impart his wisdom in a vacuum, absent any desire on the part of the leader to "seek first the Kingdom of God." Even if the Holy Spirit does provide guidance to such a leader who would otherwise have little regard for the Holy Spirit's leading, would this leader recognize it? Perhaps not. This is why Towns, Borek, and Lovett wrote,

> Christian leaders need to seek wisdom from God to gain needed insight into the appropriate course of action. This involves praying for wisdom in those areas where you lack understanding...While prayer is important, there are other things we can and should do to acquire wisdom. 'The testimony of the Lord is sure, making wise the simple' (Ps 19:7). Therefore, we should study the Scriptures regularly and receive wisdom as a by-product of that spiritual discipline.[417]

Finally, wisdom-based decision-making means little if it is not acted upon. Even the best of wisdom is pointless if the leader does not then move upon it. This is what decision-making really is all about: While the leader may seek counsel, gather inormation, and pray, he needs to finally make a decision and act upon it. Spurgeon was absolutely correct when he said,

"Brethren, do something; do something; DO SOMETHING. While committees waste their time over resolutions, do something...Too often we discuss, and discuss, and discuss, while SATAN only laughs in his sleeve. It is time we had done planning..."[418]

The hallmark of the leader is to make decisions. He can and should do so based on experience, information, intuition, and counsel. But when all is said and done, the leader called by the Holy Spirit to whatever context must always seek the Holy Spirit's guidance to fully know and do what the Holy Spirit has him leading for. Then and only then will the leader truly make effective decisions.

A Tough Decision

The toughest decision I have ever had to make as a squadron commander was when I referred a sexual assault case to an Article 32 hearing (somewhat equivalent to a grand jury in the military). The board returned it to me with a recommendation of pursuing non-judicial punishment under Article 15. This was unheard of for such as serious charge, and essentially not being able to decide for themselves what to do, they put it back on me as the commander to be the judge and jury for this case. What made it even more difficult for me was that both the accused and the victim members of my squadron. I spent hours consulting with my staff, consulting with the military lawyers, and reviewing the evidence before I made my decision, knowing that any decision I could have made would have invited massive criticism. Among my own closest staff there was disagreement as to what the right answer was, and even in my own head I was having difficulty deciding what to do. Ruling by majority might have been the easy way, but since the only signature on the Article 15 form would be mine, I knew I and only I would be accountable for the decision. After a lot of mental wrangling and prayer, I made my decision. When I informed my staff of what I intended to do, one excellent senior noncommissioned officer looked at me and quietly said, "I don't think I could ever have made a decision like you just had to make." He realized that it is one thing to offer an opinion, but quite another to make a decision that impacts people's lives to such an extent and have to take whatever criticism came. I know too that my junior officers, who were fully involved in my deliberations, saw first-hand the responsibility that would fall on them if they ever took on the responsibility of command. Whether or not my decision was right is still a matter of opinion, but seeing me have to struggle with the issue and take responsibility for the decision made a mark on my staff I could never have otherwise made.

CHAPTER 16
Courage

There is one attribute of leadership found in Scripture which is applicable in all areas yet is especially so in military leadership. All leadership involves risk-taking to some extent, yet there is no area where the costs are so high as in battle, where lives – both that of the leader and those of the followers – are at stake. Because of the extreme risks a leader faces in the military, he must have courage.

James McPherson wrote about leadership is war, "The ultimate test of leadership was combat. No officer could pass the test unless he demonstrated a willingness to do everything he asked his men to do." Indeed, it is one level of courage to send people into combat, perhaps to their deaths, but it is still another when the leader must send himself and his followers into harm's way knowing that their lives would depend on how well he functions as a leader. There is no other application of leadership where the costs of poor leadership are so extreme. The lack of courage on the part of the leader in combat is a poison to those that follow. Colonel Ardant DuPicq, who observed the Crimean Wars, wrote of leaders in battle, "If the officer is not in front of his command, it will advance less confidently... with us, all officers are almost always in advance."[419] Because the officer in front has such an impact on those following, he also advised, "He who does not feel strong enough to keep his heart from ever being gripped by terror, should never think of becoming an officer."[420]

On this one quality hang the other qualities of leadership when in combat. All others qualities are essentially a moot point if the leader then cringes under fire and cannot carry out his duties. What good are vision, wisdom, or any other attribute if the leader in the end shrinks from carrying out the mission in the face of hostility? As Carl von Clausewitz wrote, "We must never lack the calmness and firmness, which are so hard to preserve in time of War. Without them, the most brilliant qualities of mind are wasted."[421]

Clausewitz also made an excellent point that where styles in leadership may differ from leader to leader, and theories of tactics and strategy are arguable, the leader must have courage to carry out the mission. The greatest of strategists is nothing without courage, for as he wrote,

> Theory leaves it to the military leader, however, to act according to his own courage, according to his spirit of enterprise, and his self-confidence. Make your choice, therefore, according to this inner force; but never forget that no military leader has ever become great without audacity.[422]

But even without the threat of gunfire or death, every leader needs the courage to follow through on whatever vision or mission he has. Kouzes and Posner stated that it is a necessary quality in any leader; they wrote, "Having confidence and believing in our ability to handle the job, no matter how difficult, are essential in promoting and sustaining consistent efforts."[423]

What is courage really? Johnson and Harper in their book, *Becoming a Leader the Annapolis Way*, state, "The word courage stems from the French *coeur*, or heart. Thus, the expression 'take heart' is a call to courageous belief and action in the face of dismaying odds."[424] Likewise the US Army states that courage, or self-confidence, "is the faith that you'll act correctly and properly in any situation, even one in which you're under stress and don't have all the information you want."[425] Both the Army and the Navy imply that courage by its very nature involves stress and risk, and this is what distinguishes true leaders; certainly everyone wants to possess courage, but few are willing to expose themselves to the situation where they may need it.

There are also two kinds of courage, according to Oswald Sanders and to many other thinkers. Sanders wrote, "Leaders require courage of the highest order – always moral courage and often physical courage."[426] Moral courage for a leader is in knowing that he is doing what is right and that it is also essential to do. The US Air Force equates moral courage to integrity, when a person does what is right even if the stakes are high.[427] Physical courage is the bravery one has to endure pain or even death in order to accomplish a task. Neither can be equated with an absence of fear, for the lack of fear is often either ignorance of what one is facing or just pure stupidity. Courage, though, both moral and physical, deals with mastering oneself in the face of fear. The US Army wrote of it this way:

> Personal courage isn't the absence of fear; rather it is the ability

Courage When it Counted

The six months of 2008 when I was the commander of the International Zone Police in Baghdad had a dubious distinction – it was the period of the worst insurgent indirect fire attacks on the IZ since the war in Iraq began. We had 270 rocket hits in the small IZ, most of it in just two months. For everyone else in the IZ, surviving a rocket attack was a matter of getting under cover until the "all clear" sounded, but for the members of my team it was totally different – we had to be out while the rockets were coming in, attending to casualties and putting out severe fires. Every member of my team had a close call, and one rocket detonated less than fifty meters from where I was standing almost completely unprotected. All of us had to, and did, reach deep to summon the courage to do our jobs and I am deeply proud of my team to this day for literally saving lives at the risk of their own. For me, courage of this sort didn't necessarily come naturally; I had never been in life-threatening combat before and I wondered how I would handle the pressure. It would have been simple enough for me to safely stay in our control center during the rocket attacks and "lead" from there, but I couldn't do that. I knew that I had to set the tone for my team members, and I could not ask them to risk their lives if I were not willing to do so myself. I had to pray for that kind of courage, and God was faithful; I cannot explain the sense of calm and lack of fear I had, even when rockets were detonating and causing terrific damage around me, except for what David wrote in Psalm 91: "He who dwells in the shelter of the Most High will rest in the shadow of the Almighty. I will say of the LORD, 'He is my refuge and my fortress, my God, in whom I trust'...You will not fear the terror of night, nor the arrow that flies by day... A thousand may fall at your side, ten thousand at your right hand, but it will not come near you...If you make the Most High your dwelling— even the LORD, who is my refuge—then no harm will befall you, no disaster will come near your tent. For he will command his angels concerning you to guard you in all your ways; 'Because he loves me,' says the LORD, 'I will rescue him; I will protect him, for he acknowledges my name.'"

to put fear aside to do what's necessary. It takes two forms, physical and moral. Good leaders demonstrate both. Physical courage means overcoming fears of both bodily harm and doing your duty. It's the bravery that allows a soldier to take risks in combat in spite of the fear of wounds or death. Physical courage is what gets the soldier at Airborne School out the aircraft door. It's what allows an infantryman to assault a bunker to save his buddies. Moral courage is the willingness to stand firm on values, principles, and convictions—even when threatened. It enables leaders to stand up for what they believe is right, regardless of the consequences. Leaders who take responsibility for their decisions and actions, even when things go wrong, display moral courage. Courageous leaders are willing to look critically inside themselves, consider new ideas, and change what needs changing. In combat, physical and moral courage may blend together. The right thing to do may not only be unpopular but dangerous as well. Such situations reveal who is a leader of characte and who is not.[428]

As the Army stated, both types of courage blend together. In fact, both are essential in a leader because each of these qualities sustains the other; one cannot long keep one if he does not have the other. General Matthew Ridgeway wrote of how these two types of courage interact:

There are two kinds of courage, physical and moral, and he who would be a true leader must have both. Both are products of the character forming process, of the development of self-control, self-discipline, physical endurance, of knowledge of one's job and therefore of confidence. These qualities minimize fear and maximize sound judgment under pressure and – with some of that indispensable stuff called luck – often bring success from seemingly hopeless situations. Putting aside impulsive acts of reckless bravery, both kinds of courage bespeak an untroubled conscience, a mind at peace with God. An example is Colonel John H. Glenn who was asked after his first rocket flight if he had been worried, and who replied, "I am trying to live the best I can. My peace has been made with my Maker for a number of years, so I had no particular worries."[429]

Clausewitz also wrote of the interplay between moral and physical courage when wrote,

If we wage war with all our strength, our subordinate commanders and even our troops (especially if they are not used to warfare) will frequently encounter difficulties which they declare insurmountable. They find the march too long, the fatigue too great, the provisions impossible. If we lend our ear to all these difficulties, as Frederick II called them, we shall soon succumb completely, and instead of acting with force and determination, we shall be reduced to weakness and inactivity. To resist all this we must have faith in our own insight and convictions. At the same time this often has the appearance of stubbornness, but in reality it is that strength of mind and character which is called firmness.[430]

It takes strength of character and physical strength to blend into the courage so necessary for a leader in combat. Unfortunately, courage is not a natural attribute. The concept of risking oneself for another or for the sake of accomplishing a mission is generally overtaken by the natural attribute of self-preservation. Overcoming the natural tendency of self-preservation is the mark of courage. Civil War veteran John W. DeForest wrote about courage in combat, "Self-preservation is the first law of nature. The man who does not dread to die or to be mutilated is a lunatic. The man who, dreading these things, still faces them for the sake of duty and honor is a hero."[431]

Courage is not natural; fear is. It must be recognized as a law of combat that fear is the first emotion any person feels when he is preparing for or in the midst of hostility. DuPicq wrote of this human nature in combat, "Man's heart is as changeable as fortune. Man shrinks back, apprehends danger in any effort in which he does not foresee success."[432] He also stated, very plainly, that "Absolute bravery, which does not refuse battle even on unequal terms, trusting only to God or to destiny, is not natural in man."[433]

According to James McPherson, even those who were considered brave in the Civil War were just as fearful as anyone else. The only question, really, was one's response to that fear.

> But the fighters, no less than the skulkers, had to cope with the battlefield's most pervasive presence: fear. Because the conventions of masculinity equated admission of fear with cowardice, however, many soldiers were reluctant to confess what surely all felt. Some Civil War soldiers grasped intuitively, and more acquired by experience, the modern understanding that courage is not the absence of fear but the mastery of it.[434]

Indeed, all seek to overcome this natural response to danger, but it is an inherent part of the human makeup. Fear may be suppressed but it will never be disposed of entirely. Leaders will always have to deal with fear. "Man in battle," wrote DuPicq, "is a being in whom the instinct of self-preservation dominates, at certain moments, all other sentiments. Discipline has for its aim the domination of that instinct by a greater terror. But it cannot deny it completely."[435]

Yet, even if one can not totally eradicate the fear he feels in the face of danger, DuPicq hit upon a necessary element in controlling it, which is discipline. Discipline is a means by which one can moderate the natural fear, perhaps even to the extent of acting in spite of it. Discipline, according to McPherson, is what brings about courage under fire. Of it, he wrote,

> The first impulse of men under fire is an overwhelming desire to flee the danger. Many soldiers do run away, or cower into frozen immobility. But if discipline or some other factor nerves them to overcome the impulse to flight, when they go into action the flood of adrenaline turns many soldiers into preternatural killing machines oblivious to danger and fear.[436]

Just as moral courage and physical courage go hand in hand, so do the self-discipline of a commander and the discipline he imposes on those in his command. "Victory," wrote DuPicq, "belongs to the commander who has known how to keep [his followers] in good order, to hold them, and to direct them."[437] From the commander's perspective, this self-discipline must be a lifestyle and a part of his essence. This self-discipline gives him security in his ability as the leader and helps him to understand his role in leading. As DuPicq observed,

> Discipline cannot be secured or created in a day. It is an institution, a tradition. The commander must have absolutely confidence in his right to command. He must be accustomed to command and proud to command. This is what strengthens discipline in armies commanded by an aristocracy in certain countries.[438]

Discipline, for the commander, takes on a dual responsibility. He must be disciplined in himself, and he must be able and willing to discipline those in his command. "It is not enough to order discipline," DuPicq wrote. "The officers must have the will to enforce it, and its vigorous enforcement must instill subordination in the soldiers."[439]

The same is true of the commander's followers, according to DuPicq.

Discipline, he wrote, is the foundation of action under fire. "What makes the soldier capable of obedience and direction in action," he wrote, "is the sense of discipline."[440] This discipline which they have and which they also see in their leaders can help overcome the natural emotion of self-preservation and will "sustain them and prevent their fear from becoming terror."[441]

Discipline is part of the foundation for courage. But according to Clausewitz, there is yet another requirement for courage. Each person must have some compelling reason to act. There must be something which drives a leader to act which overcomes the need for self-preservation and makes him willing to act in a self-sacrificial way. Where promises of money, promotion or personal gain fail, since none of these is worth a whole lot for the leader who faces death, there must be something which drives him forward when his natural tendency is to flee. Clausewitz wrote of this compulsion,

> A powerful emotion must stimulate the great ability of a military leader, whether it be ambition as in Caesar, hatred of the enemy as in Hannibal, or pride in a glorious defeat, as in Frederick the Great. Open your heart to such emotion. Be audacious and cunning in your plans, firm and persevering in their execution, determined to find a glorious end, and fate will crown your youthful brow with a shining glory, which is the ornament of princes, and engrave your image in the hearts of your last descendants.[442]

For the leader who is called to act by the Holy Spirit, this "powerful emotion" upon which he depends to overcome his natural tendencies, is his security as a leader in the Holy Spirit. God's presence in his life, calling him to action, is what gives the Christian the courage he needs to act whether in battle or in any type of leadership challenge. Larry Michael wrote of this, "One of the greatest blessings for a leader is to know that he is in the center of God's will for his life! Such assurance brings a confidence to one's leadership…that cannot be supplied by any other motivation."[443]

So if one needs more courage, one should draw closer to God. "How can one become more confident?" asked Larry Michael. "It sounds simple but it is profoundly true: have faith in God. Draw closer to Jesus. Believe the promises of His Word!"[444]

While this sort of confidence seems more applicable to the boardroom or Sunday School type of leadership, it is just as true on the battlefield.

When a leader has disciplined himself to follow God in the calm of life, he will also find strength in the hell of battle. When a leader knows he is called by God to lead, he can take confidence that he is not acting alone. "Have I not commanded you?" God asked Joshua upon Joshua's commissioning as a leader. "Be strong and of good courage; do not be afraid, nor be dismayed, for the LORD your God is with you wherever you go" (Joshua 1:9, NKJV).[445] Is this encouragement by God to Joshua taken out of context? Indeed not; God spoke these words to Joshua prior to his attack on Jericho! This shows that this promise of God's is true on the battlefield as well as in any area of leadership.

As critical as courage is, one advantage to it is that courage is contagious. When a leader is courageous, the followers will gain courage as well. The US Navy teaches that

> Observing or reading about courage in action…often inspires others to courageous behavior as well. Followers of courageous leaders often borrow from the courage of their leaders as they face the anxiety that accompanies new challenges, unfamiliar demands, and perhaps even torture or death. In this way, a leader's stores of courage can sustain and embolden those that follow – even in the face of daunting odds.[446]

The US Army echoes those thoughts as well. The courageous leader in battle will create courageous soldiers. The Army stated,

> Self-confident leaders instill self-confidence in their people. In combat, self-confidence helps soldiers control doubt and reduce anxiety. Together with will and self-discipline, self-confidence helps leaders act – do what must be done in circumstances where it would be easier to do nothing – and convince their people to act as well.[447]

Historically this is also true. James McPherson wrote of leaders in the Civil War who, fighting in spite of their own fear, inspired the same in their soldiers. "The personal courage of officers," he wrote, "was unquestionably a powerful factor in motivating men to follow them."[448]

Biblically as well, a leader will find that courage is contagious. Oswald Sanders used Hezekiah as an example of a leader who, finding courage and strength in Yahweh, he went around to his people and encouraged them.

> Facing the ruthless armies of Sennacherib, Hezekiah made his military preparations and then set about strengthening

the morale of his people. "Be strong and courageous," he told them. "Do not be afraid or discouraged because of the king of Assyria and the vast army with him…With him is only the arm of flesh, but with us is the Lord our God to help us and to fight our battles."…Here is leadership, active and strong.[449]

Hezekiah was an interesting model. He found courage in Yahweh, but did not satisfy himself with that. His courage gave him a passion to inspire his own people. He recognized their failing spirits and took it upon himself to bolster their confidence as well.

This is why a courageous leader is so important. The followers will reflect the courage of the leader. A cowardly leader or one with a pessimistic attitude will have a negative impact on the confidence of the followers, whereas a leader who is courageous and confident will have courageous and confident followers. "Your attitude will affect the attitudes of your followers," Larry Michael wrote. "They will be confident as you are confident. Again, it comes down to influence. To exert the right influence, a leader must be positive."[450]

CHAPTER 17
Integrity

Another trait which is essential to leadership, whether in business, the church, the military or in any setting, is integrity. Integrity, like courage, is absolutely necessary in a leader since it sets the tone for the rest of the organization. If a leader wants honesty in his subordinates, he must display it himself; if a leader prefers not to act with integrity then, whether he realizes it or not, he either desires or is indifferent to a lack of it among his followers.

Integrity is a trait spoken of, but probably not fully understood. How does a leader define integrity, and therefore know it when he sees it? Integrity, in its essence, is a wholeness of self, or as the US Air Force defined it,

> Integrity is a character trait. It is the willingness to do what is right even when no one is looking. It is the "moral compass" –the inner voice; the voice of self-control; the basis for the trust imperative in today's military. Integrity is the ability to hold together and properly regulate all of the elements of a personality. A person of integrity, for example, is capable of acting on conviction. A person of integrity can control impulses and appetites.[451]

Scripture never defines integrity, but it does give some excellent examples to go by in order to understand what it is. One such example is Job. Scripture speaks of him as a man of integrity. "In the land of Uz there lived a man whose name was Job. This man was blameless and upright; he feared God and shunned evil" (Job 1:1, NIV).[452] More clearly, Eugene Peterson paraphrased that same passage to say that Job was "honest inside and out, a man of his word, who was totally devoted to God and hated evil with a passion" (Job 1:1, *The Message*).[453]

In terms of integrity in leadership, Kouzes and Posner wrote that a leader shows it through a "consistency between words and deeds."[454] This manner of integrity, they wrote, is the "ultimate test of a leader's credibility...In the doing is where leaders prove to others that they are truly serious about quality or respect or innovation or diversity or whatever the stated value."[455] When a leader's words equal the leader's deeds, then a leader has integrity.

When looking at integrity, the actions are what verify the words of a leader. A leader may never have to even speak of integrity, and yet his integrity is clear if he consistently acts with integrity. And how does a leader do this? Captain Abrashoff had an excellent prescription for integrity when he wrote,

> My self-test was simple, and it allowed me to decide whether to go or stop in terms of obvious consequences. I just asked myself this: If what I am about to do appeared on the front page of the Washington Post tomorrow, would I be proud or embarrassed? If I knew I would be embarrassed, I would not do it. If I'd be proud, I knew I was generally on the right track...And however unsophisticated it seems, as I have said before, the Sunday school standard is enough: Do the right thing. Forget petty politics, don't worry about whether you're going to upset anyone or ruffle anyone's feathers; if it is the right thing to do, figure out a way to get past the egos, a way to get round the bureaucratic infighting, and then do it.[456]

Captain Abrashoff made an outstanding point. If a leader is willing to have every action and every decision he makes completely public, fearing no shame or retribution and knowing each action will be compared to his words, then he is acting with integrity.

But is integrity really all that necessary? If quality of leadership is results-oriented, then should it really matter what it takes to get the job done so long as it gets done? If a company turns a profit, does it really matter if a few rules are broken to get there? If a commander has made his unit ready for combat or a readiness inspection, is it essential that everything was done honestly? So long as the result is achieved, cannot the ends justify the means?

Biblically, integrity is essential. Even for people in general, God insists

The Power of a Poor Example

When I got to my second Air Force assignment as a first lieutenant, a lot of the scuttlebutt was about the squadron commander getting caught with his pants down – literally. Whether it was true or not, the rumor going around was that he had been caught during a sexual encounter with his secretary. Sadly, while most of the unit was appalled, some of the senior noncommissioned officers took advantage of the situation and began having relationships with the younger Airmen in the squadron, openly and publicly. This, of course, was blatantly against rules of professional conduct but the one person who could do anything about it – the commander – was powerless to stop it. He had lost his moral authority to demand they stop because of his own illicit liaison, but he could do nothing officially either since these same people could then go to the group commander and inform on his after-hours activities. It was an appalling situation which reflected poorly on the professionalism on the entire squadron leadership, and it stuck in my mind how critical it is that a leader steadfastly guard his personal conduct. It is tough enough to demand integrity in one's followers, but when a leader compromises his own integrity it will be impossible for him to maintain it in his organization.

on integrity. "You must be blameless before the LORD your God" (Deuteronomy 18:13, NIV).[457] It does not get much more clear than this. Explaining this passage, Oswald Sanders wrote, "God wants His people to show a transparent character, open and innocent of guile."[458]

In terms of leaders, God's blessings upon them are very much tied to how they act. If a leader acts with integrity, as God told Solomon at the beginning of his reign, God himself will bless him. God was very clear that his blessings were conditional, and only if Solomon was a man of integrity would God honor him in return. "As for you, if you walk before me in integrity of heart and uprightness, as David your father did, and do all I command and observe my decrees and laws, I will establish your royal throne over Israel forever" (1 Kings 9:4-5, NIV).[459] Yet for God this was not a one-sided issue; if a leader acts with integrity, God will act in return. As Matthew Henry wrote, "On that condition the promise was made. If we perform our part of the covenant, God will not fail to perform his."[460]

When God selected leaders in Scripture, integrity was a prerequisite in addition to something a leader had to demonstrate throughout his leadership. When God was searching for a leader to replace Saul, a man of decidedly little integrity, God looked for someone with a wholeness of character; as Samuel related, "But now your [Saul's] kingdom will not endure; the LORD has sought out a man after his own heart and appointed him leader of his people, because you have not kept the LORD's command" (1 Samuel 13:14, NIV).[461] Indeed, the internal qualities of the potential leader were of far more importance to Yahweh as he searched for a new leader; as he instructed Samuel, "Do not consider his appearance or his height, for I have rejected him. The LORD does not look at the things man looks at. Man looks at the outward appearance, but the LORD looks at the heart" (1 Samuel 16: 7, NIV).[462] In the same way, Scripture dictates that leaders in the church were to be people with a demonstrated long history of integrity as well, as Paul wrote to Timothy, "Deacons, likewise, are to be men worthy of respect, sincere...They must keep hold of the deep truths of the faith with a clear conscience. They must first be tested; and then if there is nothing against them, let them serve as deacons" (1 Timothy 3:8-10, NIV).[463]

Even in non-ecclesiastical settings, integrity is very much a requirement for leaders. Kouzes and Posner wrote that integrity and honesty were the most desired qualities in leaders, not from God this time but from followers. They wrote,

> In virtually every survey we conducted, honesty was selected more often than any other leadership characteristic. Honesty is absolutely essential to leadership. If people are going to follow someone willingly, whether it be into battle or into the boardroom, they first want to assure themselves that the person is worthy of their trust.[464]

Their surveys were no anomalies. According to Larry Michael, Peter Drucker found the same sort of results. He wrote,

> Leadership expert Peter Drucker reported the results of a survey of thirteen hundred senior corporate executives. The survey revealed that integrity is the human quality most necessary to business success. Seventy-one percent of the respondents put it at the top of the list of sixteen traits responsible for enhancing an executive's effectiveness.[465]

Why is this so important? As much as a leader desires the blessing of God and should act with integrity in order to get it, a leader must also rely on the goodwill of his followers and must act with integrity to get it. Larry Michael also quoted Warren Bennis who stated,

> Leaders cannot lead effectively without the trust of their followers. When people see hypocrisy, they withhold their trust. When people are betrayed, they withdraw their support. Trusted leaders are consistent in their public and private behavior, they are authentic in their concern for their followers, and they are true to their word.[466]

Brigadier General Wakin stated that this integrity, modeled by the leader and imitated by the followers, is essential in a military setting where the demands and responsibilities are so great. He wrote,

> Integrity, obedience, loyalty—these qualities take on even more significance in the modern military as it becomes more difficult for military leaders to inculcate them in their people. The military function retains its noble and necessary role of protection of a way of life; the military profession in the United States will be equal to the task of carrying out that function only in proportion to its ability to attract and retain leaders who understand the ethical dimensions of professional competence and who themselves exemplify the highest intellectual and moral qualities.[467]

Brigadier General Wakin also quoted former Air Force Chief of Staff, General John D. Ryan, who, in a policy letter dated 1 November 1972, addressed the need for integrity in all areas of the military, both in the leaders and in the followers:

> Integrity...is the keystone of military service...Without integrity, the commander in chief cannot have confidence in us. Therefore, we may not compromise our integrity—our truthfulness. To do so is not only unlawful but also degrading. False reporting is a clear example of a failure of integrity. Any order to compromise integrity is not a lawful order. Integrity is the most important responsibility of command. Commanders are dependent on the integrity of those reporting to them in every decision they make. Integrity can be ordered but it can only be achieved by encouragement and example.[468]

If it is a responsibility of the leader to encourage and set the example for followers, then he must also ensure that he maintains it himself. Integrity can never be taken for granted; all people, whether leaders or followers, are constantly in danger of losing it. "The highest moral character," said Spurgeon, "must be sedulously maintained."[469] Indeed, he wrote, a leader must look to God to protect him from himself in order to maintain this integrity which is so vital. Spurgeon wrote,

> As you would, on bended knees, cry day and night that no moral catastrophe may occur to you, beware of the sin which leads to it, beware of the backsliding which culminates in it; for if we have not the cause, the effect will not follow. The Lord will preserve us if, day by day, we cry unto Him to cleanse our way.[470]

Yet if a leader is intent on having and maintaining his integrity, he will find the efforts worth it. When a leader has integrity, the same trust he builds with his people will filter through all levels of the organization and make it stronger, creating a climate of trust in the place of a climate of individuality and personal gain. Kouzes and Posner testified of this phenomenon,

> Clearly it is in our best interests as individuals and as leaders to be trusted by all of our constituents. If people have faith in us, our behavior will generate fewer disputes. If we don't deceive others, they will have less reason to get angry or deceive us in return. If we are reliable and others know they can count on us, then our works and actions will have greater power to influence them. If we appreciate people and show that we take their interests to heart, they can trust us to lead. People will be less suspicious and better able to deal with legitimate differences.[471]

In the end, a leader must be the one to dedicate himself to personal integrity and insist upon it within his organization. Biblically speaking, God blesses those who lead with integrity and honesty, those who not only say but do the right thing. Whether in the military or in business, or any leadership role, those who walk in integrity find that their units will do the same, and that integrity is a very strong foundation for success.

While different leadership roles may call for distinctive leadership styles, there are qualities of leaders which are essential regardless of context. Scripture shows, and it is verified through numerous secular, business and military studies, leaders must have strong families, be people of vision and competence, have the ability to make wise decisions, and possess courage and integrity. All of these must be present and none can be neglected. When a leader fails to possess any of these qualities, or if he neglects them and lets them suffer, he will find his leadership will suffer as well; yet the one who is intent on maintaining and improving each of these areas will find his leadership enhanced and his efforts proved worth while. All leaders desire these results, and none has any hope of success without these qualities firmly in place.

PART V
The Need for Leadership

The military realm is one which always requires leadership. With so much on the line, personally and nationally, military leaders must be true leaders, effective and selfless. Civil War historian James McPherson demonstrated how essential solid leadership has been in the past when he wrote,

> Studies of combat motivation focus on leadership as a key factor in the fighting effectiveness of a unit…Most Civil War soldiers would have agreed that the quality of their officers had a great deal to do with their willingness and ability to fight. They would also have agreed that the two most important criteria for a good officer were a concern for his men and leadership by example – that is, personal courage and a willingness to do anything he asked his men to do.[472]

This seems obvious for a war which included close range battles, with individual soldiers struggling with rifles and bayonets and with officers and enlisted members alike in imminent danger, but is it still true today that real leadership is essential? With such effective technology fighting our battles for us, can the military not instead focus its time and energy on other areas of officership instead of on such archaic things as leadership? Former US Army Chief of Staff, General Edward C. Meyer, insisted that to abandon the search for and development of effective leaders was not a viable option; leadership is still a must in the military in spite of the overwhelming technological capability. In fact, he insisted, the need for military leadership has not only not diminished, it has grown. "Today," he stated, "we need sensitivity and backbone beyond that which the past several decades have demanded."[473] The context of his statement makes it clear that by "sensitivity and backbone" he meant leadership.

And yet, if leadership is and has been at such a premium in the military, why are there so many misconceptions about it and what it is? Why would James MacGregor Burns have been compelled to state that, "Leadership is one of the most observed and least understood phenomena on earth"?[474]

One reason, undoubtedly, for the confusion about leadership is the study of it. The many, many studies which provide models for how one becomes a leader seem to indicate that leadership is a process or some simple steps a person can follow which invariable lead to the desired results. They attempt to create these models to encapsulate leadership without having to take into account the situation in which a person leads, the qualities of the particular leader, the qualities and motivations of the followers, the risks involved in the leadership venture, or a host of other variables. As Elmer Towns, Danny Lovett, and John Borek wrote,

> There is no one leadership trait that can be used by all people, in all situations, to lead all groups. Leadership is always expressed differently because each leader has a different personality and different strengths, and each group of followers has different needs.[475]

Because the variables of leadership are so dynamic, any "one size fits all" model of leadership is completely specious; these models completely miss the fact that leadership is a dynamic, not an equation; it is a dialogue, never a monologue; it is always a relationship and never an individual achievement. Towns, Lovett, and Borek found this thought compelling enough to write,

> A book that suggests a theoretical type of leadership is like the models that are built by automotive makers. They are snazzy but haven't proven themselves on the road. A model is how the engineers want it to run, and a leadership model is how the theorists want leadership to act. But life is not theoretical, life is encumbered with warts, memory lapses, sin, failure and non-compliant followers.[476]

For Christian leaders, this is very true. Christian leaders grow in leadership ability as their faith grows. "Human leaders are called by God to get the job done in a variety of ways," wrote Towns, Borek and Lovett. "Since none of us has arrived, all of us should be growing leaders."[477] Not only is each Christian leader forever growing as a leader and in faith, but the followers are perpetually growing and changing as well. Similarly, just as the human dynamic changes, the environment changes. Therefore, anyone who states that there is one way to lead completely misses the point that leadership styles will change as the people and the situations change. The leadership environment is in a constant state of flux, and because of this leaders cannot rely on "catch-all" models of leadership. "Leaders cannot, must not, bind themselves to a one-answer, one-method scientology," wrote General Meyer. "They must discover the method best suited to motivate and employ each soldier."[478] Leadership is truly dynamic, and no single model can capture every dynamic.

In addition to the confusion over inappropriate leadership models, there is a tendency to look at leadership and management as being synonymous. Yet this is just as grave an error as creating strict leadership models. As General Meyer adamantly stated, "Leadership and management are neither synonymous nor interchangeable."[479] Equating the two concepts is ridiculous as well as damaging. Unfortunately, though, the current trend in military thinking either disagrees with General Meyer's statement and sees leadership and management as one and the same, or sees management as a greater virtue to the extent that the military is marginalizing leadership in favor of business-style management. This does not imply at all that management or management practices are without place in the military; to the contrary, they are of great importance. The vast personnel, budget, and logistical issues any military unit faces make it clear that leaders need to use good management practices to make a unit more efficient. The problem, though, is that even exceptional management alone cannot now and never will be able to achieve success on the battlefield. "Managers can put the most modern and well-equipped force into the field," stated General Meyer pointedly. "They cannot, however, *manage* an infantry unit through training or *manage* it up a hill into enemy fire to seize an objective" (italics in original).[480] Only what US Air Force Lieutenant Colonel Donald R. Baucom called the "heroic leader" can gain victory in war, and that heroic leader, he says, is becoming a rarity in the military.

> The balance [between heroic leadership, military managers, and the military technologist] is being disrupted by several factors that are eroding the respect traditionally accorded the heroic leader within the military profession; with its decline comes a deterioration of the warrior spirit he embodies. These factors are the all-volunteer force, a civilianization of

157

American military institutions and activities, an overemphasis on management, and an enthrallment with technology.[481]

Indeed, Lieutenant Colonel Baucom stated, the military is currently functioning like a business far more than like the traditional military, partly because of the need to attract recruits like a business would attract workers. Those who are not motivated by patriotism or a sense of service must be attracted and retained in other ways; hence the military has essentially become a business in which its leaders are expected to behave more like CEOs or salespeople. "Having been forced to recruit like a business and therefore attracting people motivated by marketplace incentives," Lieutenant Colonel Baucom wrote, "the military naturally drifts toward the management practices used by private industry."[482]

The result of this, then, is that commanders who formerly were to focus on preparedness and battlefield capability now need to concern themselves with issues more traditionally in the managerial realm. The cost of this is a loss in military expertise and leadership ability, according to Lieutenant Colonel Baucom. As he stated, "In an all-volunteer force [AVF] environment, then, officers must devote more time and effort to coping with the AVF, and less time to the study of their profession and to the preparation of their units for war."[483]

So as the military becomes increasingly obsessed with budgets, analyses, and metrics, management becomes the primary virtue of military commanders at the expense of leadership. In fact, the vernacular of the military in recent times seems to indicate that the military expects leaders to manage their units to victory in war instead of lead them as Lieutenant Colonel Baucom noted,

> Terms such as battle management, battle manager, levels of management, resource management, weapons inventory, weapons systems, and management by objective proliferate throughout the Air Force. Such management functions as budgeting and productivity improvement are pushed down to the lowest operational level – the traditional domain of the heroic leader – where they compete for the commander's time and energy, often at the cost of essential and time-honored command functions.[484]

The result, then, is a perception—if not a reality—that officers need to choose between leadership skills and management skills if they are to advance in their careers. If there is not enough time for both, then the officer needs to sacrifice one to succeed and advance; the institutionalized choice is to sacrifice leadership. "Systems analysis, combined with management training," wrote Lieutenant Colonel Baucom, "has become the primary path to the top for officers."[485]

While the business-like model of management has taken primacy, Lieutenant Colonel Baucom noted another disturbing trend which has made real leaders an even more endangered species: Leaders are being replaced by technologists. What was once the domain of brilliant strategists is now becoming the place of computer models. It is as if the military can find a program for victory instead of leading its forces to it. He pointed out that,

> The impact of this view of war obviously is to raise the stature of military technologists and military managers who are responsible for developing, procuring, and sustaining the wonder weapons of war. The importance of warriors and heroic leaders, as we have noted, is diminished. "Operating a console in an air-conditioned electronic listening post becomes equivalent to facing a T72 tank with a handheld missile."[486]

Again, this is not to diminish the importance of those who find and acquire the technology to assist the military leader in the fight; in fact, the technology in the military today has had a great role in reducing battlefield casualties and has had a proven role in making the warrior-commander more effective in leading. And yet, the trend is not to enhance warrior-leaders through technology but to replace them, and as machine-minded managers come to the forefront, their abilities to motivate and inspire people to achieve a goal becomes of secondary importance if of any importance at all. As technology has become the darling of the military, personal leadership skills have eroded greatly.

Management and technology tended to replace leadership especially as nuclear weapons became the staple of the military strategy. If mutually-assured destruction was the only option to not fighting at all, then it is no wonder Bernard Brodie observed that, "Thus far the chief purpose of our military establishment has been to win wars. From now on its chief purpose must be to avert them. It can have almost no other useful purpose."[487] This frame of mind certainly would see battlefield leaders as a relic which should be replaced by businessmen, and yet the last fifteen years have demonstrated that human combat is still a necessary skill for the military; technology alone has not been able to defeat terrorism—in fact, terrorists are exceptionally adept in being able to beat technology—and managerial fads are rendered useless in combat. Clearly then, the battlefield leader is still necessary in the military, far more so than managers and technologists.

So if leadership and management are not synonymous, then what really is military leadership? The US Army states that, "Leadership is influencing people – by providing purpose, direction, and motivation – while operating to accomplish the mission and improving the organization."[488] Lieutenant Colonel Baucom defined it in the same way, that "[t]o lead has clear connotations of influencing behavior by example, by being out front, by going before: to 'lead the way, to go in advance of others…to be at the head of, command, direct.'"[489] More specific to the leader in combat, the US Army wrote,

> Military leadership is a process by which a soldier influences others to accomplish the mission. Leaders coordinate the other three elements [maneuver, firepower, protection] of combat power. Their competent and confident leadership results in effective unit action. The right leadership gives purpose, direction, and motivation in combat. Leaders must know their profession, their soldiers, and the tools of war. Only this kind of leadership can direct soldiers to do difficult tasks under dangerous and stressful conditions.[490]

If the distinction is not clear here between military leadership and management, note that nothing is said in any of these definitions of being able to set agendas or organize staff meetings, balance a budget or analyze processes. Are these necessary functions in an organization? Yes, but not so much in the leader. The leader's function is to determine where the organization is to go, set the course, and motivate the people to follow him there. That is leadership in its essence; this is what is so necessary today.

Thomas Cronin summarized the difference well. He wrote, "Managers are concerned with doing things the right way. Leaders are more concerned with identifying and then getting themselves and their organizations focused on doing the right thing."[491] Leaders certainly need managers to develop and maintain processes for getting things done, but management without leadership is merely motion with no direction; it is activity without motivation. A unit without good management may be disorganized, but a unit without good leadership is pointless.

So there must be a clear distinction which separates leaders from managers, and there must then be a greater emphasis on leadership. "In the long run," Morris Janowitz wrote, "the military establishment cannot be controlled and still remain effective by civilianizing it…the professional soldier is, in the last analysis, a military commander and not a business or organizational administrator."[492] If it is not the military institution which will emphasize this, then it is the leaders who must take it upon themselves to learn to lead and not just to manage. They must study leadership and, more importantly, exert themselves to practice it. They must seek out opportunities to be leaders, not just to hold a leadership role and then move on. "Is it the quality of staffs or that of combatants that makes the strength of armies?" asked Colonel Ardant DuPicq. "Do they say that military science can only be learned in the general staff schools? If you really want to learn your work, go to the line."[493] The only way to be a good leader is to practice it.

Parenthetically, while there is a trend to confuse leadership with management, there is also a dangerous trend in the "how-to" manuals which insist a leader must be of a particular personality. They often prescribe a perpetually happy, excitable person who is capable of arousing the adrenaline of the followers and get the job done. This, too, is a fallacy, as Richard and Henry Blackaby point out:

> Collins and Porras, in their book *Built to Last*, concluded that the contention that 'visionary companies require great and charismatic visionary leaders' is a myth. On the contrary, they are determined that 'a charismatic visionary leader is absolutely not required for a visionary company and, in fact, can be detrimental to a company's long-term prospects.' Great leaders, they discovered, built great organizations, not necessarily great reputations. When organizations are built around the personality of a leader, not only is the organization susceptible to the weakness and whims of the leader, but it also faces an inevitable crisis when the leader leaves the organization…Personality without purpose and charm without competence are recipes for ruin. [Leaders] who function more on personality than on true leadership qualities rarely stay in one place for long.[494]

Leadership must not be built on a foundation of personality. True, the job of a leader is to motivate followers, but it must be a greater motivation than just excitement. As Lieutenant Colonel Baucom wrote of military leadership, "In exercising leadership, the commander must at times compel his followers to undertake actions that may not be in their own best interests."[495] True; self-sacrifice may be the lot of those in combat, and that certainly is not in one's own best interests. Is it imaginable, then, that a leader should get his followers excited, thrilled, and "pumped up" about charging into an enemy line or flying into heavy air defenses, knowing some of them will probably die? This is not leadership; this is psychotic. It may the leadership of a kamikaze or jihadist perhaps, but never the leadership in a society which values human life. If this is the case then a leader cannot motivate simply out of charisma.

There is, then, a need for real leadership beyond management and personality, and it is appropriate for leaders to turn to Scripture in order to understand what a leader is. Whether civilian or military, a leader should comprehend the Biblical precepts which demonstrate what the Holy Spirit desires of leaders he anoints. It may seem odd to turn to the Holy Bible as a study for military leadership, but Scriptural leadership is very applicable even to the military setting. Retired US Air Force Major General William Cohen gave a case in point when he used Gideon's attack on the Midianites as a great example of military leadership, and one as applicable today as ever. "This special operation force was so successful," he wrote, "that even today the Israeli Army considers Gideon's raid the model for its commando operations."[496] So why not turn to Scripture for an understanding of military leadership? According to the Blackabys many do, but oddly it is not the Christian leaders who are doing so. "Incredibly," they wrote, "as secular writers are embracing Christian teachings with the fervency of first-century Christians, Christian leaders are inadvertently jettisoning many of those same truths in an effort to become more contemporary!"[497] It seems as thought the people who have not realized this truth are Christian leaders themselves!

So what does Scripture require of those called to lead others? First, and without this a leader is hopeless, a leader should seek an intimacy with God. With all of the demands placed on leaders and all of the requirements a person must fulfill in order to be effective, a leader must strive to know and understand God above all else. Does a military officer or any person desire to have the abilities and qualities of a good leader? If so, he should "seek first the kingdom of God and his righteousness, and [then] all these things will be added to [him]" (Matthew 6:33, NKJV).[498] If a leader makes it his top priority to seek God and know him, then God will never fail to equip him to do the work which God has called him to do.

That equipping which God promises, or "power" according to Acts 1,[499] comes to a leader in the form of the Holy Spirit. Every military leader called by God to lead in that context should understand and take comfort that when leaders are faithful to God, the Holy Spirit will manifest himself in them to make them more effective and bring glory to God. Military leaders need not worry so much about how the Holy Spirit shows himself— the ways he does are as varied as the situations in which he will do it—but need only be faithful to the calling the Holy Spirit gives. In doing so, leaders will find themselves far more effective in both the temporal and eternal aspects of leadership, both in accomplishing the military mission and fulfilling the Great Commission as well.

When one accepts the role of a leader appointed by the Holy Spirit, he must realize as well that the leadership he assumes is not for his benefit or aggrandizement but for the benefit of those he leads, and that success as a leader will come at a tremendous personal cost. The Holy Spirit does not call a person to leadership to glorify that person and make his life easy, but rather to serve others by leading them. In doing so, a leader must reject self-centered leadership and be ready to sacrifice himself, his own status, and his own ambition for the good of those he leads and for the sake of the calling of the Holy Spirit. Yet a leader called in such a way knows that the cost he pays to lead effectively will yield a greater reward, perhaps not so much for himself immediately, but for that which is truly important and which is greater than the leader himself.

Scripture is very clear that leaders must have the qualities of putting their families first and ensuring their vitality, of being competent in the job they perform, of having a vision for the future of the organization, of making wise decisions, of courage, and of integrity. These demands, clearly indicated in Scripture, are the foundations upon which a leader must build his own style or method of leading. Should the leader allow any of them to erode, he will find his leadership compromised as well. Scripture requires each of these qualities in leaders, and many are verified by secular sources as well. For instance, James Kouzes and Barry Posner testified that,

> More than 1500 managers nationwide provided 225 values, characteristics, and attitudes that they believed crucial to leadership. A panel of researchers and managers subsequently analyzed the factors and reduced them to fifteen categories. The most frequent responses, in order of mention, were 1) integrity (Leaders are truthful, are trustworthy, have character, have convictions), 2) competence (leaders are capable, productive,

efficient); and 3) leadership (leaders are inspiring, are decisive, provide direction). A follow-up study sponsored by the Federal Executive Institute Alumni Association, involving eight hundred senior public sector administrators, replicated these findings.[500]

These surveys show there is a great demand for these qualities in leaders, to the exclusion of many of the managerial competencies that so many leadership studies prescribe. A leader should see these as evidence that their personal qualities are of far more importance, and deserve far more attention, than any method or style of leadership ever will be.

To state it again, there is a need for leadership—especially Scripture-based leadership—in all disciplines but especially in the military. If Samuel P. Huntington is correct that the real distinction between civilian leadership and military leadership is the management of violence,[501] then how much more so should military leaders learn and rely on the leadership principles of Scripture? In any other realm of leadership, success and failure can be determined by the quality of leadership, but in the military it is more than just success and failure; it is often literally the difference between life and death. A person called by the Holy Spirit to serve as a leader in the military should make it an obsession to let the Holy Spirit have a profound impact first on his life and second on his abilities as a leader; he must never attempt to lead without the influence of the Holy Spirit in either aspect. Such a leader must also see past the temporal goals of the organization, however important, and allow the Holy Spirit to make a truly eternal difference in the lives of those he leads. The leader can take solace in knowing he is not called to preach but to lead, and when he leads in the power of the Holy Spirit he will find that the Holy Spirit will impact his followers at whatever point of discipleship they are and bring them to a greater knowledge and understanding of Almighty God.

In conclusion, Biblical leadership is not a matter of "how to do"; a person simply cannot be an effective leader by following a recipe or blueprint. Rather Biblical leadership is a matter of "how to be." A leader is forever in pursuit of a greater intimacy with God; a leader always subjects his life to the Holy Spirit to show and glorify God in the world; a leader lives a life of sacrifice to those he leads; and a leader constantly exerts himself to build and maintain a solid foundation of Biblical qualities on which he can stand. When a leader lives these things, then he is living the life of leadership.

Bibliography

Abrashoff, D. Michael, (CAPT, USN). 2002. *It's Your Ship: Management Techniques from the Best Damn Ship in the Navy.* New York: Warner Books.

American Heritage Dictionary of the English Language, Fourth Edition. 2000. Houghton Mifflin Company.

Amplified Bible, The. 1987. The Lockman Foundation.

Barton, John and John Muddiman, ed. 2001. *Oxford Bible Commentary.* Oxford: Oxford University Press.

Be, Know, Do: Leadership the Army Way: Adapted from the Official Army Leadership Manual. 2004. San Francisco: Jossey-Bass.

Bereit, Rick. 2002. *In His Service: A Guide to Christian Living in the Military.* Colorado Springs: Dawson Media.

Blackaby, Henry T and Melvin, 2004. *What's So Spiritual About Your Gifts?* Sisters: Multnoma Publishers.

Blackaby, Henry T and Richard. 2001. *Spiritual Leadership: Moving People on to God's Agenda.* Nashville: Broadman and Holman Publishers.

Borek, John, Danny Lovett, and Elmer Towns. 2005. *Good Book on Leadership: Case Studies from the Bible.* Nashville: Broadman and Holman.

Bugbee, Bruce. 2005. *What You Do Best in the Body of Christ.* Grand Rapids, Zondervan.

Carson, D.A., 1987. *Showing the Spirit: A Theological Exposition of 1 Corinthians 12-14.* Grand Rapids: Baker Book House.

Cohen, William A. 2006. *Special Ops Leadership: Dare the Impossible, Achieve the Extraordinary.* New York: AMACOM.

Doyle, Arthur Conan. 2004. The *Adventures and Memoirs of Sherlock Holmes.* New York: Sterling Publishers.

Elwell, Walter A. ed. 1989. *The Marshall Pickering Commentary on the NIV.* London: Baker Book House.

Erikson, Millard J. 1998. *Christian Theology, Second Edition*. Grand Rapids, Baker Books.

Field Manual 7-8, *Infantry Rifle Platoon and Squad*. 22 April 1992, Headquarters Department of the Army: Washington DC.

Flynn, Leslie B. 2004. *19 Gifts of the Spirit*. Colorado Springs: Cook Communications Ministries.

Getz, Gene. 1995. *David: Seeking God Faithfully*. Nashville: Broadman and Holman Publishers.

Goldfein, David L. 2001. *Sharing Success, Owning Failure: Preparing to Command in the 21ˢᵗ Century Air Force*. Maxwell Air Force Base: Air University Press.

Graham, Billy. 1988. *The Holy Spirit*. United States: W Publishing Group.

Grudem, Wayne. 1994. *Systematic Theology: An Introduction to Biblical Doctrine*. Grand Rapids: Zondervan.

Guinness, Os. 1998. *The Call: Finding and Fulfilling the Central Purpose of Your Life*. Nashville: Word Publishing.

Gutherie, D. and J.A. Motyer. 1970. *The New Bible Commentary, Revised*. Carmel: Guidepost.

Henry, Matthew. 1984. *The NIV Matthew Henry Commentary in One Volume*. Grand Rapids: Harper Collins.

Hybels, Bill. 2002. *Courageous Leadership*. Grand Rapids: Zondervan.

Johnson, W. Brad and Gregory P. Harper. 2005. *Becoming a Leader the Annapolis Way: Twelve Combat Lessons from the Navy's Leadership Laboratory*. New York: McGraw-Hill.

Kouzes, James M. and Barry Z. Posner. 2003. *Credibility: How Leaders Gain It and Lose It, Why People Demand It*. San Francisco: Jossey-Bass.

Lester, Richard I. and Glenn A. Morton, ed. 2001. *Concepts for Air Force Leadership*. Maxwell Air Force Base: Air University Press.

Maxwell, John C. 2002. *The Maxwell Leadership Bible*. Nashville: Thomas Nelson, Inc.

Maxwell, John C. 2000. *The 21 Most Powerful Minutes in a Leader's Day*. Nashville: Thomas Nelson, Inc.

Maxwell, John C. 1998. *The 21 Irrefutable Laws of Leadership*. Nashville: Thomas Nelson, Inc.

McPherson, James M. 1997. *For Cause and Comrades: Why Men Fought the Civil War*. Oxford: Oxford University Press.

Meyer, John G. Jr. 1990. *Company Command: The Bottom Line.* Fort Lesley J. McNair: National Defense University Press.

Michael, Larry J. 2003. *Spurgeon on Leadership: Key Insights for Christian Leaders from the Prince of Preachers.* Grand Rapids: Kregel Publications.

Peterson, Eugene H. 2002. The *Message: The Bible in Contemporary Language.* Colorado Springs: NavPress.

Puryear, Edward F. Jr. 2000. *American Generalship: Character is Everything: The Art of Command.* New York: Ballantine Books.

Roots of Strategy, Book 2. 1987. Mechanicsville: Stackpole Books.

Ryrie, Charles Caldwell. 1994. *The Ryrie Study Bible: New International Version.* Chicago: The Moody Bible Institute.

Sanders, J. Oswald. 1994. *Spiritual Leadership.* Chicago: Moody.

Stanley, Charles F. 2005. *Living the Extraordinary Life: Nine Principles to Discover It.* Nashville: Nelson Books.

Stanley, Charles F. 1999. *Ministering through Spiritual Gifts.* Nashville: Thomas Nelson, Inc.

Taylor, Robert L. and William E. Rosenbach, ed. 1984. *Military Leadership: In Pursuit of Excellence.* Boulder: Westview Press.

United States Air Force Core Values, 1 January 1997.

Warren, Rick. 2002. *The Purpose Driven Life: What on Earth Am I Here For?* Grand Rapids: Zondervan.

www.askoxford.com/worldofwords/quotations/quotefrom/mallory/

ABOUT THE AUTHOR

Paul D. Cairney is a lieutenant colonel in the United States Air Force. He grew up in Colorado Springs, Colorado, and graduated from the US Air Force Academy Preparatory School in 1988 as a Distinguished Graduate. In 1992 he graduated from the US Air Force Academy with Military Distinction and a Bachelor of Science Degree in Military History. He has served eighteen years as a security forces officer in various assignments in North Dakota, Turkey, Nevada, the United Kingdom, Colorado, Germany, and Louisiana. He has commanded two security forces squadrons, one of which was selected as Outstanding Medium Security Forces Squadron in Air Force Space Command for 2005. He also served six months as the commander of the International Zone Police in Baghdad during Operation *Iraqi Freedom*, where he earned the Army Combat Action Badge and the Bronze Star Medal for combat leadership. He earned a Master of Arts in Religion Degree from Liberty Baptist Theological Seminary in September 2002 and a Doctor of Philosophy Degree in Leadership from Louisiana Baptist University in 2007. He is married to the former Lynn Thompson of Sacramento, California, and together they enjoy spending time training and riding their horses.

ENDNOTES

1. John C. Maxwell, *The Maxwell Leadership Bible.* (Nashville: Thomas Nelson, Inc., 2002), 1183.

2. Eugene H. Peterson, *The Message: The Bible in Contemporary Language.* (Colorado Springs: NavPress. 2002), 1363.

3. Walter A. Elwell, ed. *The Marshall Pickering Commentary on the NIV.* (London: Baker Book House. 1989.), 750.

4. Elwell, 750.

5. Elwell, 750.

6. Henry, 119.

7. Ryrie, NIV, 1744.

8. Henry, 594.

9. Henry, 594.

10. Elwell, 950.

11. John Barton and John Muddiman, ed. *Oxford Bible Commentary.* (Oxford: Oxford University Press, 2001), 1104.

12. D. Gutherie and J.A. Motyer. *The New Bible Commentary, Revised.* (Carmel: Guidepost. 1970.), 1039.

13. Peterson, *The Message*, 1557.

14. Ryrie NIV, 1744.

15. Peterson, *The Message*, 1557.

16. Ryrie,1744.

17. Henry, 595.

18. Ryrie,1744.

19. Blackaby, *Gifts*, 13.

20. Blackaby, *Gifts*, 14.

21. Blackaby, *Gifts*, 18.

22. Blackaby, *Gifts*, 20.

23. John Borek, Danny Lovett, and Elmer Towns. *Good Book on*

Leadership: Case Studies from the Bible. (Nashville: Broadman and Holman, 2005),126.

24. Rick Bereit. *In His Service: A Guide to Christian Living in the Military.* (Colorado Springs: Dawson Media, 2002), 73.

25. Bereit, 74.

26. Os Guinness. *The Call: Finding and Fulfilling the Central Purpose of Your Life.* (Nashville: Word Publishing, 1998), 31.

27. Blackaby, *Gifts,* 29.

28. Rick Warren. *The Purpose Driven Life: What on Earth Am I Here For?* (Grand Rapids: Zondervan, 2002), 177.

29. Charles F. Stanley. *Living the Extraordinary Life: Nine Principles to Discover It.* (Nashville: Nelson Books, 2005), 59.

30. J. Oswald Sanders. *Spiritual Leadership.* (Chicago: Moody, 1994), 28.

31. Borek, 126.

32. John C. Maxwell. *The 21 Irrefutable Laws of Leadership.* (Nashville: Thomas Nelson, Inc., 1998), 11.

33. James M. Kouzes and Barry Z. Posner. *Credibility: How Leaders Gain It and Lose It, Why People Demand It.* (San Francisco: Jossey-Bass, 2003), xv.

34. Sanders, 19.

35. Borek, 125.

36. Hybels, Bill. *Courageous Leadership.* (Grand Rapids: Zondervan. 2002), 189.

37. Borek, 126

38. Sanders, 44.

39. W. Brad Johnson and Gregory P. Harper. *Becoming a Leader the Annapolis Way: Twelve Combat Lessons from the Navy's Leadership Laboratory.* (New York: McGraw-Hill, 2005), 75.

40. *Be, Know, Do: Leadership the Army Way: Adapted from the Official Army Leadership Manual.* (San Francisco: Jossey-Bass, 2004), 25.

41. *Leader to Leader,* 21.

42. Ryrie NIV, 315.

43. Borek, 117.

44. Pickering, 138-139.

45. Borek, 119.

46. Henry, 227.

47. Ryrie NIV, 425.

48. Borek, 148.

49. Gene Getz. *David: Seeking God Faithfully.* (Nashville: Broadman and Holman Publishers, 1995), 27.

50. Sanders, 18.

51. Henry, 382.

52. Maxwell, NKJV, 524.

53. Peterson, *The Message*, 545-546.

54. Pickering, 281.

55. Maxwell, NKJV, 531.

56. Henry, 484.

57. Barton, 291.

58. Maxwell, NKJV, 533.

59. Peterson, *The Message*, 554.

60. Henry, 486

61. Maxwell, NKJV, 544.

62. Ryrie, NIV, 675.

63. Barton, 299.

64. Maxwell, NKJV, 545.

65. Peterson, *The Message*, 566.

66. Maxwell, NKJV, 550.

67. Henry, 1189

68. Ryrie, NIV, 315.

69. Peterson, *The Message*, 275.

70. Henry, 221.

71. Stanley, *Life*, 47.

72. Sanders, 86.

73. Stanley, *Life*, 47.

74. Sanders, 92.

75. Larry J. Michael. *Spurgeon on Leadership: Key Insights for Christian Leaders from the Prince of Preachers.* (Grand Rapids: Kregel Publications, 2003), 23

76. Borek, 108.

77. Johnson, 1.

78. Henry, 221.

79. Ryrie, NIV, 940.

80. Ryrie, NIV, 1902.

81. Kouzes, 60.

82. Kouzes, 52, 60.

83. Peterson, *The Message*, 275.

84. Henry, 221.

85. Michael, 61.

86. Michael, 99.

87. Borek, 111.

88. Sanders, 19.

89. Blackaby, *Gifts*, 39.

90. Michael, 37.

91. Sanders, 19.

92. Henry T and Richard Blackaby. *Spiritual Leadership: Moving People on to God's Agenda.* (Nashville: Broadman and Holman Publishers, 2001), 100.

93. Stanley, *Life*, 59.

94. Blackaby. *Spiritual Leadership* 31.

95. Henry, 629.

96. Ryrie, NIV, 1770.

97. D.A. Carson. *Showing the Spirit: A Theological Exposition of 1 Corinthians 12-14.* (Grand Rapids: Baker Book House, 1987), 35.

98. Billy Graham, *The Holy Spirit.* (United States: W Publishing Group, 1988), 167-168.

99. *The American Heritage Dictionary of the English Language, Fourth Edition* (Houghton Mifflin Company: 2000)

100. Carson, 34.

101. Peterson, *The Message*, 1578.

102. *The Amplified Bible* (The Lockaman Foundation: 1987)

103. Blackaby. *Spiritual,* 11.

104. Bruce Bugbee, *What You Do Best in the Body of Christ.* (Grand Rapids: Zondervan,2005). 52.

105. Ryrie, NIV, 1836.

106. Sanders, 83.

107. Bugbee, 52.

108. Sanders, 28.

109. Blackaby, *Gifts,* 82.

110. Michael, 68.

111. Blackaby, *Spiritual Leadership*, 141.

112. John C. Maxwell, *The Maxwell Leadership Bible.* (Nashville: Thomas Nelson, Inc., 2002), 1402.

113. Graham, 168.

114. Michael, 216.

115. Wayne Grudem. *Systematic Theology: An Introduction to Biblical Doctrine.* (Grand Rapids: Zondervan, 1994), 1016.
116. Carson, 41.
117. Maxwell, NKJV, 1405.
118. Blackaby. *Spiritual Leadership,* 180.
119. Blackaby, *Spiritual Leadership,* 13.
120. Stanley, *Life,* 78.
121. Warren, 242.
122. Blackaby. *Gifts,* 17.
123. Maxwell, NKJV, 1381-1382.
124. Maxwell, NKJV, 338.
125. Maxwell, NKJV, 339.
126. Blackaby, *Spiritual Leadership,* 18.
127. Henry, 466.
128. Maxwell, NKJV, 506.
129. Blackaby, *Gifts,* 19.
130. Millard J Erikson. *Christian Theology, Second Edition.* (Grand Rapids, Baker Books, 1998), 897.
131. Henry, 595.
132. Maxwell, NKJV, 526.
133. Maxwell, NKJV, 527.
134. Henry, 595.
135. Henry, 595.
136. Ryrie, NIV, 1770-1771.
137. Graham, 201.
138. *Roots of Strategy, Book 2: Three Military Classics.* (Mechanicsville: Stackpole Books, 1987), 317.
139. David L. Goldfein. *Sharing Success, Owning Failure: Preparing to Command in the Twenty-First Century Air Force.* (Maxwell Air Force Base: Air University Press, 2001), 9.
140. Michael, 67.
141. Blackaby, *Spiritual Leadership,* 20.
142. Blackaby, *Gifts,* 23.
143. *United States Air Force Core Values,* 1 January 1997. 6.
144. Maxwell, NKJV, 1195.
145. Bereit, 97.
146. Maxwell, NKJV, 1393
147. Peterson, *The Message,* 1567.
148. Bereit, 93.

149. Maxwell, NKJV,1440.
150. Leslie B. Flynn, *19 Gifts of the Spirit*. (Colorado Springs: Cook Communications Ministries, 2004), 21.
151. Bereit, 100.
152. USAF Core Values, 11.
153. Goldfein, 14-15.
154. John G. Meyer, Jr. *Company Command: The Bottom Line*. (Fort Lesley J. McNair: National Defense University Press, 1990), 7, 9.
155. Michael, 31.
156. Henry, 226.
157. Grudem, 868.
158. Maxwell, NKJV, 1300.
159. Blackaby, *Spiritual Leadership*, 127.
160. Blackaby, *Spiritual Leadership*, 76.
161. Maxwell, NKJV, 1403.
162. Maxwell, NKJV, 1404.
163. Maxwell, NKJV, 1404.
164. Henry, 631.
165. Sanders, 29.
166. Graham, 174.
167. Flynn, 29.
168. Blackaby, *Gifts*, 30.
169. Blackaby, *Spiritual Leadership*, 94.
170. Henry, 78.
171. Blackaby, *Gifts*, 20-21.
172. Blackaby, *Gifts*, 48.
173. Borek, 126.
174. Sanders, 23.
175. *Be, Know, Do*, 79.
176. Warren, 255.
177. Robert L. Taylor, and William E. Rosenbach, ed. *Military Leadership: In Pursuit of Excellence*. (Boulder: Westview Press. 1984), 71-72.
178. Blackaby, *Gifts*, 82.
179. Erikson, 897.
180. Blackaby, *Gifts*, 23.
181. Blackaby, *Gifts*, 42-43.
182. Blackaby, *Gifts*, 44.
183. Blackaby, *Gifts*, 43.

184. Maxwell, NKJV,1256.

185. Sanders, 115.

186. John C. Maxwell, *The 21 Most Powerful Minutes in a Leader's Day.* (Nashville: Thomas Nelson, Inc. 2000), 297.

187. Michael, 32.

188. Sanders, 116.

189. Charles F. Stanley. *Ministering through Spiritual Gifts.* (Nashville: Thomas Nelson, Inc., 1999), 77.

190. Blackaby, *Spiritual Leadership,* 19.

191. Maxwell, NKJV, 86.

192. Maxwell, NKJV, 284.

193. Meyer, 7.

194. Sanders, 117, 119.

195. Maxwell, NKJV, 1476.

196. Meyer, 8.

197. Taylor, 73.

198. Sanders, 14.

199. Kouzes, 232.

200. Borek, 26.

201. Sanders, 119.

202. Maxwell, NKJV, 1476.

203. Blackaby, *Spiritual Leadership,* 158.

204. Sanders, 116.

205. Johnson, 2.

206. Sanders, 18.

207. Blackaby, *Spiritual Leadership,* 90.

208. Maxwell, NKJV, 1183.

209. Peterson, *The Message,* 1364.

210. Ryrie, NIV, 1542.

211. Sanders, 21.

212. Sanders, 21.

213. Michael, 29.

214. Graham, 174.

215. Blackaby, *Spiritual Leadership,* 231.

216. Tozer in Sanders, 29-30.

217. James M. McPherson, *For Cause and Comrades: Why Men Fought the Civil War.* (Oxford: Oxford University Press,1997), 55.

218. Bereit, 117.

219. Sanders, 61.

220. Arthur Conan Doyle. *The Adventures and Memoirs of Sherlock Holmes*. (New York: Sterling Publishers, 2004), 488.
221. Henry, 595.
222. Blackaby, *Spiritual Leadership*, 91.
223. Ryrie, NIV, 1857.
224. Meyer, 3, 5.
225. Henry, 595.
226. Bereit, 133-134.
227. Maxwell, NKJV, 1519.
228. Maxwell, NKJV, 1432.
229. Peterson, *The Message*, 1610.
230. Ryrie, NIV, 1795.
231. Henry, 648.
232. Warren, 205.
233. Ryrie, NIV, 1795.
234. Maxwell, *21 Minutes*, 254.
235. Michael, 46.
236. Michael, 46-47.
237. Michael, 155.
238. Maxwell. *Irrefutable*, 189.
239. Meyer, 7.
240. Taylor, 91.
241. Kouzes, 186.
242. Kouzes, 185.
243. Sanders, 15.
244. Kouzes, 7.
245. Bereit, 118.
246. Bereit, 121.
247. Bereit, 123.
248. Kouzes, 31.
249. Ryrie, NIV, 1646.
250. Blackaby, *Spiritual Leadership*, 167.
251. *Be, Know, Do*, 48.
252. Meyer, 15, 11.
253. Blackaby, *Spiritual Leadership*, 165-166.
254. D. Michael Abrashoff (CAPT, USN). *It's Your Ship: Management Techniques from the Best Damn Ship in the Navy*. (New York: Warner Books, 2002), 13.

255. William A. Cohen. *Special Ops Leadership: Dare the Impossible, Achieve the Extraordinary.* (New York: AMACOM, 2006), 37.
256. Cohen, 37.
257. Michael, 30.
258. Kouzes, 46.
259. Kouzes, 97-98.
260. Meyer, 25.
261. Kouzes, 100.
262. Kouzes, 192.
263. Bereit, 134.
264. Taylor, 87.
265. Blackaby, *Spiritual Leadership*, 139.
266. Kouzes, 54.
267. Kouzes, 185
268. Meyer, 8.
269. Kouzes, 9.
270. Blackaby, *Spiritual Leadership*, 107.
271. Blackaby, *Spiritual Leadership*, 97.
272. Kouzes, 30.
273. Kouzes, 9.
274. Kouzes, 187.
275. Blackaby, 168.
276. Abrashoff, 6.
277. Bereit, 117.
278. Maxwell, NKJV, 1183.
279. Ryrie, NIV, 1824.
280. Kouzes, 19.
281. AF Core Values, 6.
282. Blackaby, *SpiritualLeadership*, 88.
283. Sanders, 148.
284. Sanders, 13.
285. Bereit, 47.
286. Maxwell, NKJV, 1158.
287. Peterson, *The Message*, 1338.
288. Maxwell, NJKV, 269.
289. Blackaby, *Spiritual Leadership*, 142.
290. Bereit, 159.
291. Meyer, 8.
292. Sanders, 14.

293. Ryrie, NIV, 1135.
294. Ryrie, NIV, 1748-1749.
295. Ryrie, NIV, 1906-1907.
296. Sanders, 14.
297. Sanders, 15.
298. Blackaby, *Spiritual Leadership*, 100.
299. Sanders, 16.
300. Ryrie, NIV, 1567.
301. Bereit, 43.
302. Sanders, 15.
303. Bereit, 43.
304. Blackaby, *Spiritual Leadership*, 111.
305. Ryrie, NIV, 318.
306. Ryrie, NIV, 366.
307. Blackaby, *Spiritual Leadership*, 96.
308. Ryrie, NIV, 1468.
309. Blackaby, *Spiritual Leadership*, 98.
310. Maxwell, NKJV, 696.
311. Maxwell, NKJV, 769.
312. Bereit, 47.
313. Ryrie, NIV, 405.
314. McPherson, 23.
315. McPherson, 131.
316. Meyer, 8.
317. Meyer, 8.
318. Maxwell, NKJV, 1476.
319. Peterson, *The Message*, 1641.
320. Michael, 124.
321. Blackaby, *Spiritual Leadership*, 253.
322. Sanders, 43.
323. Maxwell, NKJV, 227.
324. Henry. 203.
325. Bereit, 45.
326. Sanders, 44.
327. Maxwell, *Minutes*, 29.
328. Maxwell, *Minutes*, 30.
329. Ryrie, NIV, 270.
330. Michael, 121.
331. Michael, 121.

332. Michael, 23.
333. Kouzes, 17.
334. *Be, Know, Do,* 10.
335. Taylor, 59.
336. Meyer, 13-14.
337. Bereit, 38.
338. Michael, 23.
339. Grudem. 1024.
340. Kouzes, 73.
341. Grudem, 1022.
342. Kouzes, 74.
343. *Be, Know, Do,* 12.
344. Sanders, 103.
345. Sanders, 109.
346. *Be, Know, Do,* 12.
347. Hybels, 31.
348. Kouzes, 16.
349. Goldfein, 23-24.
350. Goldfein, 23
351. Kouzes, 25.
352. Abrashoff, 9.
353. Goldfein, 51.
354. Blackaby, *Spiritual Leadership,* 58.
355. www.askoxford.com/worldofwords/quotations/quotefrom/ mallory/
356. Blackaby, *Spiritual Leadership,* 60.
357. Ryrie, NIV, 1819.
358. Peterson, *The Message,* 1617.
359. Maxwell, NKJV, 48.
360. Maxwell, NKJV, 48.
361. Maxwell, NKJV, 351.
362. Ryrie, NIV, 1500.
363. Blackaby, *Spiritual Leadership,* 23-24.
364. Blackaby, *Spiritual Leadership,* 68.
365. Michael, 96.
366. Blackaby, *Spiritual Leadership,* 69.
367. Blackaby, *Spiritual Leadership,* 63.
368. Ryrie, NIV, 822-823.
369. Blackaby, *Spiritual Leadership,* 47.

370. Blackaby, *Spiritual Leadership*, 70.
371. Blackaby, *Spiritual Leadership*, 59.
372. Blackaby, *Spiritual Leadership*, 60.
373. Blackaby, *Spiritual Leadership*, 66-67.
374. Blackaby, *Spiritual Leadership*, 69.
375. Blackaby, *Spiritual Leadership*, 71.
376. Michael, 31.
377. Cohen, 73.
378. Ryrie, NIV, 289-290.
379. Ryrie, NIV, 224.
380. Goldfein, 28-29.
381. Blackaby, *Spiritual Leadership*, 75.
382. Hybels, 38.
383. Borek, 26.
384. Michael, 94.
385. Goldfein, 95.
386. Blackaby, *Spiritual Leadership*, 111.
387. Hybels, 32-33.
388. Borek, 27.
389. Blackaby, *Spiritual Leadership*, 168.
390. Kouzes, 168.
391. Borek, 49.
392. Sanders, 58.
393. Sanders, 59.
394. Edward F. Puryear, Jr. *American Generalship: Character is Everything: The Art of Command.* (New York: Ballantine Books. 2000), 67.
395. Field Manual 7-8, *Infantry Rifle Platoon and Squad* (Headquarters Department of the Army: Washington DC, 22 April 1992), 1-3.
396. Sanders, 57.
397. Cohen, 17-18.
398. Abrashoff, 9.
399. Borek, 49.
400. Goldfein, 30.
401. Cohen, 16-17.
402. Maxwell, NKJV, 285.
403. Borek, 118.
404. Maxwell, NKJV, 1519.
405. Maxwell, NKJV, 518.

406. Henry, 474.
407. Blackaby, *Spiritual Leadership*, 179.
408. Maxwell, NJKV, 747.
409. Henry, 595.
410. Ryrie, NIV, 957
411. Blackaby, *Spiritual Leadership*, 197
412. Blackaby, *Spiritual Leadership*, 249.
413. Blackaby, *Spiritual Leadership*, 244.
414. Blackaby, *Spiritual Leadership*, 190.
415. Blackaby, *Spiritual Leadership*, 193.
416. Borek, 170.
417. Michael, 32.
418. *Roots*, 145.
419. *Roots*, 146.
420. *Roots,* 317.
421. *Roots*, 318.
422. Kouzes, 167.
423. Johnson, 84.
424. *Be, Know, Do*, 34.
425. Sanders, 59.
426. *United States Air Force Core Values*, 1 January 1997. 5.
427. *Be, Know, Do*, 29.
428. Taylor, 25.
429. *Roots*, 368.
430. McPherson, 5.
431. *Roots*, 144.
432. *Roots*, 120.
433. McPherson, 36.
434. *Roots*, 77.
435. McPherson, 40.
436. *Roots*, 127.
437. *Roots,* 137.
438. *Roots*, 248.
439. *Roots,* 148.
440. *Roots,* 146.
441. *Roots,* 373.
442. Michael, 35.
443. Michael, 38.

444. Maxwell, NKJV, 242.
445. Johnson, 83-84.
446. *Be, Know, Do*, 35.
447. McPherson, 60.
448. Sanders, 61.
449. Michael, 40.
450. *AF Core Values*, 5.
451. Ryrie, NIV, 751.
452. Peterson, *The Message*, 635.
453. Kouzes, 47.
454. Kouzes, 185.
455. Abrashoff, 39.
456. Ryrie, NIV, 288.
457. Sanders, 62.
458. Ryrie, NIV, 516.
459. Henry, 392.
460. Ryrie, NIV, 419.
461. Ryrie, NIV, 425.
462. Ryrie, NIV, 1855.
463. Kouzes, 14.
464. Michael, 84.
465. Michael, 77.
466. Wakin, 63.
467. Wakin, 180.
468. Michael, 85.
469. Michael, 85-86.
470. Kouzes, 112.
471. McPherson, 53.
472. Taylor, 80.
473. Taylor, 79.
474. Borek, 26.
475. Borek, 3.
476. Borek, 2.
477. Taylor, 83.
478. Richard I. Lester and Glenn A. Morton, ed. *Concepts for Air Force Leadership*. (Maxwell Air Force Base: Air University Press, 2001), 19.
479. Taylor, 81-82.

480. Lester, 17.
481. Lester, 18.
482. Lester, 24.
483. Lester, 24.
484. Lester, 19.
485. Lester, 21.
486. Lester, 21.
487. *Be, Know, Do,* 5.
488. Lester, 20.
489. FM 7-8,1-2d.
490. Taylor, 96.
491. Lester, 26.
492. *Roots,* 238.
493. Blackaby, *Spiritual Leadership,* 91-93.
494. Lester, 20.
495. Cohen, 13.
496. Blackaby, *Spiritual Leadership,* 11.
497. Maxwell, NKJV, 1158.
498. Maxwell, NKJV, 1315.
499. Kouzes, 12.
500. Lester, 26.